Meditational Self-Care

A Manual

Daniel Chapelle

ISBN: **1540577538**

ISBN 13: **9781540577535**

Library of Congress Control Number:

2016919959

SittingDuckPublishing

Boston, MA

Contents

Acknowledgment

True wisdom is nobody's property. It belongs to all of humanity. The author acknowledges a debt of gratitude to a multitude of writers, both contemporary and past—in many cases reaching back centuries, even millennia. There is no way to repay this debt, other than by trying to further the understandings gained from this host of prior writers.

With one or two exceptions the only writer cited here by name is the modern Western philosopher Friedrich Nietzsche. His philosophy is the only one that compares in scope, reach, insight, and depth with that of the Eastern meditation tradition, whose primary teacher is the Buddha.

"We love life not because we are used to living but because we are used to loving."

— Nietzsche

Why meditate?

Meditation can loosen the grip of personal unhappiness, no matter what your situation or your history is. It can dissolve heavyheartedness and make for more lightheartedness, deep contentment, and love of existence.

Meditational self-care is a practice more than a theory. It revolves around a core of views or ideas that go beyond therapeutic psychology, which is only a little over a century old and which has largely failed to improve human lives. Meditational self-care joins modern psychology with the multi-thousand-year-old tradition of meditation.

That tradition has a proven record of producing happier souls. The merging of these two traditions works like the botanical art of grafting. There two different plants are joined to grow together. They become one and produce a new fruit with the desirable characteristics of both plants.

Meditational self-care differs from psychotherapy in three important ways. First, it is not something that one person does to another. It is a gradually and slowly learned skill. It can be likened to learning how to play a musical instrument. In meditational self-care, just as in learning to play a musical instrument, a teacher provides instruction and continuing guidance but it is we, the students, who must do all the practicing.

The second difference is even more important than the first. Traditional psychotherapy has focused mainly on reducing what it considers abnormal experiences and behaviors. It has little to say about the normal unhappiness that is an essential aspect of existence, even under the best of circumstances. It has tended to believe that all it can do is reduce the misery of mental disorders to normal everyday forms of unhappiness and then leave people to fend for themselves. In contrast, meditational self-care, like the meditation tradition, is aimed precisely at the normal and seemingly unavoidable unhappiness of existence.

The third difference is the one that matters most. Western psychology tends to attribute personal unhappiness mostly to unsatisfactory circumstances and to unsatisfactory events from our life and history. Meditational self-care views unhappiness differently. It regards the beliefs that we hold about our personal self as the primary source of all unhappiness. That is why its leading principle and starting point can be summed up this way: "We suffer from who we think we are." Meditational self-care liberates us from the hold that these beliefs about ourselves have on us and that turn our mind into a self-made prison.

Personal ideas we cling to in order to feed and support our self-image work like a monkey trap. This consists of a coconut or a gourd with a small hole in it and with some food placed inside. The monkey reaches in and closes his fist around the food. This makes his fist too big to pull it out. It does not occur to the monkey to let go of the food. Instead, he clings to it. He is now stuck. He has become a prisoner and his own prison guard. He does not realize that he has become his own worst enemy. Personal beliefs we cling to in order to feed and support our self-image work in the same way.

Modern psychotherapy has begun to realize something about this mental monkey trap. It says, "Don't believe everything you think." That is an excellent start, but it does not go far enough. It does not complete the job of overcoming the very habit and process that create the normal unhappiness of everyday life. Meditational self-care, like the meditation tradition, makes a giant leap beyond this limited first step. It does not just say: "Don't believe everything you think." It says: "Don't believe *anything* you think."

Learning to make this giant leap frees us not only from the impact of specific unhappy-making beliefs. It frees us from the very habit and process of becoming identified with all the thoughts that arise in our mind. It stops those thoughts from becoming beliefs that bind us like a monkey trap. Meditational self-care amounts to training our monkey mind in the practice of letting go.

We alone have the power to break the spell of personal ideas to which we cling like a monkey clinging to the food in its trap. We alone can transform our personal unhappiness into lightheartedness, deep contentment, and cheerfulness. Every human life is capable of these, because they are inborn. That natural lightheartedness, deep contentment, and cheerfulness remain accessible at any time. They are accessible no matter what our situation and history may be.

Meditational self-care teaches a series of practices. Anyone can learn and apply them in his or her life. It is independent of our circumstances and of our social, cultural, intellectual, philosophical, ideological, religious, or spiritual orientation. It is a technology of mind, a practical psychology for everyday living. It is not a religion. It is not a set of ideas that need to be believed. It is not a doctrine to which we must subscribe.

Learning meditational self-care is a gradual process. As already mentioned, it is like learning to play a musical instrument. It requires the three p's of practice, persistence, and patience. The first fleeting indications of potential benefits may begin to appear surprisingly quickly. They also pass away quickly. Their greatest significance is that they show glimpses of what is possible. This serves as motivator to stick with the practice. Over time the indications of potential benefits grow clearer. Their implications and significance become more convincing. They keep on multiplying and magnifying as long as we continue to practice. That practice is meant to take us through our entire life— through all our experiences of successes and seeming failures, through all setbacks and losses great and small. It also takes us through sickness, aging, and the inescapable ending of life.

This teaching is kept simple in order to make it as clear as possible, easy to follow, and workable in any life. But simple is not the same as simplistic. The teaching condenses and concentrates the active ingredients of many subtle and complex issues from centuries and millennia of philosophy, meditation practice, and psychology. All it takes to benefit from learning to practice meditational self-care is the strong intention and the sustained motivation to exchange personal dissatisfaction with existence for more of a lighthearted cheerfulness about it.

The teaching is also and deliberately kept brief. It is not meant to display a mass of information. The total volume of material that is contained in this book or that comes out of it is not measured by the number of its pages, by references, or by the amount of factual information. It is measured in the amount of personal experience the reader pours into it that is then transformed into firsthand insight. This is a manual for living, not an academic dissertation. If there is nothing new in it—and there is not—that is a virtue, not a shortcoming, because it is concerned with time-tested practical wisdom. Great traditions need to be taught again and again, and in new ways. That is how they stay alive. This book is an attempt to say and teach old things in new and, hopefully, useful ways.

How to use this manual

The practices in this manual are preceded by the views or ideas on which they are based. They turn those views into direct experiences. Both the views and the practices must be repeated again and again, as in learning to play a musical instrument. How much you learn and how much you gain depends on how much you practice and how long you sustain your practice. For best results you need to practice as close to everyday as possible, and to keep on doing so throughout your life.

It is perhaps a good idea to first read the entire series of views and practices at least once. That way you become somewhat familiar with them, so that you do not have to wonder about what is going to come next.

This is especially the case for the practices. The first time you learn about them you can just read what is in the practices without actually doing them. Then go back over the material and start doing the practices. Remember that this program is about a way of being. It is not just information, or some ideas to merely think about for a while. It is meant to change the quality and the experience of your existence by changing the way you live.

Once you have some idea about each of the views and practices it is perhaps best if you then take a more systematic and disciplined approach. You could, for example, devote an entire week to just one practice before you move on to the next. Start with the first and work your way toward the last.

After you gain some familiarity with doing the practices and after you begin to understand something about the views underlying them you can start to develop your own style. For each new day in your ongoing engagement with this program you can then begin by focusing on the particular practice that seems to best suit your mind-state and your need of the moment. Learn to observe where you are at mentally and to take the temperature of your state of mind at that moment. Then begin by focusing on the practice that most fits it—but without ever ignoring the other views and practices. Make sure that you diligently cover all the practices and that you keep spending time on the views underlying them. That way you will learn something new every time, even if you thought you understood all there is to each view and each practice.

Do not leave out any view or practice, do not give any one of them short shrift, and do not treat any one of them with preference, because that will limit and stop your progress. With time, and as you will discover for yourself, the views and practices together become one view and one practice. Even the artificial dividing line between view and practice will begin to fade.

The views and practices become one skill—one art of more contemplative everyday living for the sake of a more deeply contented and lighthearted way of being. As time goes on you will learn where and how to start on any given day, with which practice and view. You will learn what to emphasize in your practice of the day. And, like the notes and phrases of a piece of music, the elements of your practice will begin to blend.

1

We suffer from who we think we are: Who do you think you are?

View

Every form of unhappiness—whether small or great, brief or long, physical or mental, understandable or seemingly irrational—all of it is the result of what and how we think about ourselves. But even beyond that, it is the result of the very belief that there is a solid personal self to think about in the first place. That is why the core idea of meditational self-care is this: We suffer from who we think we are. Practically speaking this means that, whenever we are unhappy, we should examine, on the spot, who we think we are at that very moment.

The example of a woman with a history of lapsing into recurring depressed moods illustrates what is at stake. She had been in psychotherapy off and on, and she had eventually also taken up a meditation practice. One day she made a startling discovery: "My mind is making me miserable." These were the exact words with which she reported her discovery. It is the same discovery that the Buddha made and that every unhappy soul eventually has to make before things can begin to turn around.

Notice that there are three parts to what the woman said—and what she said goes for all of us. First there is "My mind..." Second there is "making me..." And third there is "miserable." The first, "My mind," is about her discovery that it was not her job, her marriage, her history, or any other external factor that was making her miserable, as she had long believed. It was her own mind that was making her miserable.

The combination of the second and third part of what she said—"making me" and "miserable"—talks about her discovery of a process, an activity of her "mind." This "making me" says that what she calls "me" is made, namely by her "mind." Just like this woman, we—all of us—do not just exist as we think we do or as we think we are. We do not just *be*. We *become*. We are "made," and by nothing other than the activity of our "mind." And how are we being made? How do we turn out in this making process? We are, more often than we care, being made unhappy—courtesy of our own mind.

The woman's discovery did not magically make her unhappiness go away. But it did mark a turning point, just as it did with the Buddha. It marked a sort of emotional point of no return. This point of no return made it impossible to continue to believe that it was the external factors of her life and history that were periodically making her depressed. Something very important was at stake in this discovery.

We can begin to better understand what is at stake by starting with an imaginary question-and-answer.

Q: Imagine yourself surrounded by wolves. What do you do?
A: Stop imagining.

Most of us have never been surrounded by wolves, and most of us are never going to be surrounded by wolves. And yet, without realizing it, we are constantly imagining, instead of soberly perceiving, the situations in which we find ourselves.

We naturally, spontaneously, and inevitably think and talk in fanciful ways as we engage in this process. At the same time we fail to realize that we are being fanciful and driven by our imagination. Much as we may believe otherwise, there is no way around this image-based way of thinking and talking. We have become experts at it without even trying, and without realizing it. And so, for example, we have no difficulties with understanding expressions like "feeling antsy" or "being dog tired" or feeling "surrounded by wolves."

These and similar ways of talking and thinking are not just occasional. They are not just isolated figures of speech. We are constantly imagining things without realizing that we are using a figurative language. All language is always figurative. Things cannot be otherwise. There is no such thing as an imagination-free situation, an imagination-free event, or an imagination-free experience. That is because there is no such thing as imagination-free language and imagination-free perception and thinking. There is, as Nietzsche put it, no such thing as immaculate perception.

These imaginings shape not only how we think and feel about everything we experience. They also, and before anything else, shape how we think and feel about ourselves. Because of that they also shape how we react at every moment of our life. For that reactivity is based on what we believe about ourselves and about the situation of the moment.

We only have to take a closer look at our routine daily behaviors in order to get a glimpse of just how much this is happening. For it happens all the time—all day long, day in and day out, every day of our life, until our last day and our last breath.

Picture yourself on an ordinary day as you are at home and getting ready to go into the world and do what you normally do. Look closely at this familiar routine and at this familiar picture of yourself. Notice that while you are getting ready, you are not only putting on your clothes and straightening your hair. You are also putting on the personal habits, mannerisms, and attitudes for your familiar role in your life. You have a pretty good idea of what it means to be you and not someone else. You also have a good idea of how you would like to appear, both in your own eyes and in the eyes of the world around you.

Notice that as you put on your clothes and gather your things you are also mentally preparing yourself for the situations you expect to be dealing with that day. You have some ideas about how you would like to see yourself handle your day, about what you would like to say and do, and about what you would like to see happen in response to your actions. So far so good.

And then you walk out the door. Chances are that soon after you walk out the door things begin to turn out differently than expected. On an especially difficult day it may even feel like nobody or nothing in the world seems to agree with what you had in mind.

What you are routinely doing in all the normal preparatory imagining before you enter the stage of your day is a universal human activity. It is the universal human activity of telling yourself who you think you are.

Shakespeare has a character who represents this activity of self-imagining. His name is Bottom. He appears in *A Midsummer Night's Dream*. That play is about a series of dream-like events that take place one summer night. It is full of characters who are involved in all manner of unpredictable and sometimes seemingly irrational activities—perhaps not unlike much of normal everyday life itself. Bottom, who is one of these characters, goes through his own share of experiences. When he wakes up from the night's activities he is utterly bewildered by what has been happening. He is like all of us at those times when we feel bewildered by something that has happened in our life.

When Bottom awakens he intuitively knows, just as all of us naturally do at every moment of our life, that it is important to formulate some sort of account of the events and of himself in them. He and we need this in order to gain a sense of clarity about what we have experienced and about our personal identity.

Bottom, as Shakespeare portrays him, feels too befuddled to come up with such an account by himself. And so he turns to another character in the play. He turns to a figure named Peter Quince, who is a poet and songwriter in the play. Bottom wants Peter Quince to tell him the story of who he is and of what he has experienced. He wants a story that he can then tell himself and everyone else. And the story has to be good enough for Bottom to want to live in it. He wants what the American folksinger Melanie said we all want: "I wish I could find a good book to live in." Bottom is Everyman or Everywoman in search of a good story to inhabit. And Peter Quince is for Bottom the answer to that search. He personifies the universal human behavior of telling our life to ourselves.

When things go well for us we are both Bottom and Peter Quince, simultaneously. At those times we are telling our life to ourselves as we are living it—and we believe every word of what we tell ourselves. But when things do not go our way and we become bewildered by our experiences then we are like Bottom and we lose the capacity to tell our life to ourselves. And then, like Bottom, we may feel a need for help. For many people in the modern westernized world this eventually means going into psychotherapy. And there, just like Bottom, we hope to find a sort of designated editor of the story of our life. We hope to find a Peter Quince with a license to tell us who we are. We give that figure permission not only to tell us who we are and what we should believe about who we are. We also want this editor of our life to tell us how we should act based on that account and that belief.

Whenever the story we tell ourselves about ourselves is challenged by what actually happens we become lost in confusion. This can range from a passing and minor feeling of irritation to a dramatic experience that changes everything about who we think we are. Depending on our temperament and on the extent of the confusing experience we may perhaps adjust without difficulty at all. Or we may become impatient or annoyed or angry.

We may even feel totally devastated. This is where the course of our life and our future is decided.

In the normal course of everyday life there are ultimately only two options that seem to matter to us. Either things go our way and as we like, making us want more of the same, or things do not go our way, which is something that we dislike and that makes us react accordingly. Meditational self-care begins precisely here, at this point where things are not going our way and as we had imagined.

The question we must learn to ask is this: Precisely who is being impatient with the unexpected turn of events? Who feels annoyed or angry? Who is surprised and disappointed by the way things are turning out? Who feels betrayed? Who believes him-

or herself to be the wounded party? And what exactly is that wounded party's complaint? Finally and most importantly, who is now taking over and taking charge of the situation? Who is deciding on the reaction plan? And on the basis of what belief is that reaction plan being formed? What is the underlying idea in the dislike of the situation and in the reaction to it? Who is shaping and orchestrating the reactivity that is set in motion and that defines and shapes our unhappiness?

In meditational self-care we handle these questions by as it were assuming the role of a forensic sketch artist. But here it is not, as is usually the case, in order to draw a picture of a suspect. It is, instead, to draw a picture of the injured party. More precisely, it is to draw a picture of the personal self-image that is being challenged in the unhappy-making turn of events.

In meditational self-care we learn how to do this sketch artist work for ourselves. This involves developing the clearest possible picture of our habitual unhappiness patterns. For we are most uniquely who we are and we are most identifiable in the precise ways in which we shape our unhappiness. And that, in turn, is determined by how we imagine our unhappiness.

The purpose of this process is to gain a clearer picture of who we think we are and of the personal beliefs underlying that self-image. For if all unhappiness is the result of who we think we are then the first step away from that same unhappiness is to become more conscious and clear about who we think we are.

This is what the Buddha meant when he described his enlightenment as a liberating awakening from mind-made unhappiness. This awakening frees us from the unhappiness-driven reactivity that comes with imaginings of threats to our usual self-image. Ultimately it is about our monkey mind learning to let go of what it is tightly holding on to and of what entraps it in a state of imprisonment.

Practice

Close your eyes. Bring to mind a situation or an event that involves familiar feelings and thoughts of unhappiness. If you like you can use a situation or event from the past, or you can use unhappy feelings and thoughts you may be having at this very moment. Use your capacity to clearly bring to mind this felt experience. Then just let it be as it is, without trying to comment on it, judge it, analyze it, or do anything about it. Be like a host who receives a guest just as the guest presents him- or herself. This open and nonjudgmental receptivity is vital, not only in this first practice but throughout this entire program.

Then begin to ask variations on the kind of questions a forensic sketch artist might ask a witness to an event. Ask: Who exactly is feeling the unhappiness—or the anger, the neediness, the hostility, or whatever it is you may be experiencing? Who is doing the thinking as you are feeling the unhappiness? Who is doing the complaining? What exactly is the complaint? Who has the impulse to react in the way that you would really like to react to this unhappiness?

Be as precise as you can but be nonjudgmental. You are only playing the role of a sketch artist here. You are not in a courtroom. You are not the accuser, the defendant, the judge, the jury, or the executioner. You are only creating a mirror image, not a mug shot. This is not judgment day. Make it, rather, nonjudgment day. Meditational self-care is intended precisely to learn how to make every day nonjudgment day.

Keep at this practice of the sketch artist until you have the clearest possible picture of the suffering party and its complaints. The clearer you can make this picture the easier it becomes to see something that is vital. It becomes possible to see that not all of you is unhappy and suffering. It becomes possible to see that not all of you is unhappy and suffering all the time, or even now. Only one self-image is unhappy and suffering right now. But that one self-image right now is taking over. It would make you believe that it is all of who you are, and that it is so always. But it is not. It only tempts you to think it is.

When you have a clear picture of the suffering self-image, stand back and look at it. See if you can create a mental distance from that self-image. See if you can generate a felt sense of mental space around it. That way it does not take up and take over all of you and all of your world and your existence.

Notice what happens when you practice like this, when you are getting a clear picture of the suffering self-image and when you step back to take a good look at it from an observing distance. What happens is that the original sense of unhappiness and suffering begins to diminish. It may even begin to dissolve altogether. The sense of suffocation that is part of the unhappiness of the moment taking over all of you begins to diminish. It begins to decrease to the extent that you can gain some distance from it and to the extent that you can begin to develop a felt sense of mental space around it. The unhappiness is now no longer all there is to you. You are more like that larger and truly boundless space than you are like the claustrophobic small prison space of your unhappiness.

When you begin to experience this relief from unhappiness by developing a sense of space around it, sit with that feeling of relief and of space for a few moments. Let it sink in. Dwell in the felt sense of space and of the relief it brings.

After a few moments or minutes of mentally dwelling like this you can open your eyes. Look at everything around you. Notice that you are now looking with refreshed eyes. You are now more free of the distorting and unhappy-making beliefs and habits of thinking with which you started this practice session. Look at all the familiar and ordinary things that surround you—but without naming or providing any commentary or judgment about what you see. Take your time for this looking around with refreshed eyes. Take a few moments or minutes of just looking around and seeing what you see, with nothing else to do.

Looking at familiar and ordinary things in this way helps to consolidate the felt sense of relief from the unhappiness with which you started. When you look at everything around you this way you will no longer feel that you are surrounded by wolves. Instead, you will begin to feel a certain lightness, a subtle touch of quiet and peace, as well as deep contentment.

Just continue to look at everything around you, without thinking and without silently talking to yourself. Simply acknowledge everything that is there, without naming anything and without adding any kind of thought elaboration. Just notice what you see: walls, decorative items, plants, colors, furniture, a lamp on a desk, a door, paper and paper clips, and whatever else there is.

The objective here is nothing more, but also nothing less, than to just recognize and acknowledge the presence of everything that is there. You will find yourself beginning to look and see with a recovered and refreshed sense of amazement, simple but powerful amazement that all these things are there at all. When you were a baby you looked at everything this way, and you were awed by everything you saw. But then, as you grew up and began to tell yourself a story about yourself, you started forgetting how to do this. Now you can rediscover and relearn how to do this.

You can tell that you are practicing this as intended when you find that you are experiencing a sense of subtle but real admiration and delight about everything. That includes admiration and delight about things as unassuming as a paper clip, a pen, or whatever else is right in front of you— even your own hands and fingers. You may find yourself spontaneously smiling about the mere and sheer presence of everything. You may even find yourself almost wanting to burst into laughter when you recover this ability to see with fresh eyes. If you do feel this urge to burst into laughter, then you will understand something about the easy laughter of a baby or a young child, or the smile and the childlike laughter of long-term meditators. It is the same laughter you experienced when you were a baby. Sit with it. Enjoy it. Make it last.

2

The core practice: Willing suspension of all beliefs about yourself

View

If unhappiness results from believing who we think we are then the remedy is to become aware of and to stop believing in who we think we are.

There is nothing wrong with any thoughts that arise, no matter what their content is. In any case, we cannot control what thoughts do arise. Unhappiness starts not with the thoughts themselves but with believing them. And that is something we can control. The skill to be learned is the skill of suspending the habit of believing everything we assume or tell ourselves about ourselves. Hence the focus of this second practice, which is the core practice of this entire program: willing suspension of all beliefs about yourself.

This is where meditation enters into play. The how-to of meditation is largely a matter of learning the practice of paying close attention to being here, now, in this precise moment, in the circumstance at hand, and with the felt experience just as it is. We learn to do this without adding any commentary, without adding a story, and without making any kind of judgment. It also means refraining from focusing on the past or the future. Meditation is about practicing willing suspension of belief in all that we normally, habitually, reflexively, and compulsively tell ourselves about our experiences. It is a practice of freeing ourselves from habitual forms of personal unhappiness by refraining from automatically believing everything we think. That means especially becoming free of everything we think about ourselves without even being aware of it.

In normal everyday life we tend to be where we are not. We tend to think about the past, or about the next thing, or about some time after that. We naturally and habitually practice being where we are not by imagining ourselves elsewhere. We imagine ourselves in a situation that is not taking place at this moment, in circumstances that are different from those at hand, and in a time other than now. This spontaneous and natural form of being where we are not is made possible and made compulsive as a result of who we think we are, who we think we want to be, and how we think the world should therefore treat us.

The cure for the unhappiness that comes with this lies in learning and practicing to be where we actually are. This is always here, always now, always in the circumstances of this moment, and always experiencing whatever it is we are experiencing right now, and not something else. This is easier said than done, especially on an ongoing basis and while we go through our daily activities.

Being here, now, with this experience of this moment is the great challenge for which meditation practice is the method of choice. It is a challenge that eventually has to be taken up from moment to moment. It takes a great deal of practice, persistence, and patience to learn how to be here and now. For here and now is a place where we may not have been in a long time. For many of us it is a place where we have not been since we were young children. It tends to be a forgotten experience. It has become unknown or unexplored territory. It is a territory we tend to avoid. How do we avoid it? By thinking about other things, in other places or different circumstances, and at a time that is not now.

Ancient maps of the world indicated unexplored territories with the warning words "Here live lions" or "Here be dragons." While there may be little unexplored territory left in the physical world the core anxiety that is expressed by the words "Here live lions" or "Here be dragons" is still with us. For many of us it is an almost constant presence. It can be like a virtual double that serves as our constant companion. But the anxious mental state that is the issue here is not about lions or dragons but about what goes on in our minds.

It is natural for endless things to appear in our minds. There is an endless stream of awareness. From moment to moment these endless things come and go. Nothing ever stays. Nothing remains unchanged. Few of the things that appear are lions or dragons. But when we anxiously expect or fear to see them or some other danger we are distracted from seeing what is actually there. That includes especially what appears in the internal environment of our mind and in its spontaneous activity at the moment. We tend, instead, to worry about something in the future or to ruminate about something in the past.

We are, all of us, habitual and compulsive thinkers. We habitually and compulsively think about everything, nearly all the time. For many it is virtually impossible to stop thinking even for a moment, let alone a longer stretch of time. But paradoxically, while we think about everything we encounter and experience, we may be paying very little close attention to any of it. And so we listen without hearing, we look without seeing, we grasp without feeling, we eat without tasting, and so on. We prefer to think rather than to pay attention.

Thinking allows us to reduce something that is new and unknown to something that is presumably already known. Thinking, in this respect and in this context, is the hallmark and the defining habit of anxious people. They are constantly afraid of encountering something new and previously unknown. And we are all naturally inclined to be anxious. In contrast, paying close attention to something before beginning to think about it is the sign of openness, fearlessness, and good faith. It shows a readiness to be not only surprised but potentially also filled with admiration, with awe, and, who knows, possibly even with cheerful delight. Paying attention is about becoming aware that everything is just so, as it is, and not otherwise.

The bulk of the natural unhappiness of existence is largely the result of too much unnecessary thinking. As one contemporary spiritual teacher put it, we are, quite literally, lost in thought. That is what we have learned to make of the human condition. We have become lost in thought out of ever-present fear. We believe it is imperative to think all the time out of perceived necessity for the sake of survival. Freedom from the unhappiness of existence comes from overcoming excessive thinking. That, in turn, begins with the practice of paying close and meticulous attention to things as they are before we start thinking about them.

To be here, now, and not somewhere else at some other time and in some other situation sounds simple. It may sound simple but it is neither simplistic nor easy. It is something we have to learn and practice before we can become good at it. The meditation tradition is the world's oldest, most time-tested, and surest way to treat our existential attention-deficit disorder. It trains the mind to be present as witness to all experiences that appear in awareness in just the way they do.

Paying close attention to experiences is a natural form of practicing true intimacy—intimacy with the world and with our own life. Some have said that paying close attention is the soul's natural mystical prayer. We do not have to believe in a soul, we do not have to be religious or a mystic, and we do not have to put any stock in prayer to understand what this means.

Everyone knows of experiences in which looking really closely at something, with intense interest and without agenda, can unexpectedly lead to epiphanies of wonder. Those epiphanies of wonder may be triggered by things great or small. They can be occasioned by things that are spectacular or by things that may seem insignificant. They may even happen in the presence of things that are not necessarily pleasant but that may be quite unpleasant. And most dramatically, the usual notions of good and bad, or good and evil, spontaneously go out the window when we practice true and deeply intimate attention.

The meditation tradition's discipline of paying close attention and of developing open and receptive alertness is the core element, the active ingredient, in meditational self-care. Practice it well, as often as you can, and you will be rewarded with the wonders of the world that are everywhere and always present, even on the worst day of your life.

Practice

Sit down on a chair or a meditation cushion. Sit with dignity, with your back straight but not straining. Imagine a string attached to the crown of your head, gently pulling up and straightening your back. Let your hands rest in your lap or on your legs.

Listen to the instructions that follow with an open and receptive mind. Refrain from getting caught up in analyzing the instructions, or from silently arguing about them, or from engaging in a monologue of your own. This is a practice of wordlessly experiencing, not intellectualizing and verbalizing. It is not an academic exercise but a practical skill for living. Make sure your mind is set right for this. That means open, receptive, and welcoming.

In the rest of this practice session and in all future sessions, periodically check your posture. This simplest of practices—sitting with dignity, with your back straight but not straining, and with open and receptive awareness—this is the most important part of the entire training program. It is the foundation for your liberation from mind-made unhappiness. Periodically checking your posture is especially helpful when you discover that your alertness has been dull or that your mind has been wandering unchecked for a long period of time. Practice it well, and over time you will discover that it provides a basis for a growing pleasure in just sitting, with nothing else to do.

You can either close your eyes or keep them partly open. If you keep them open do so with an unfocused gaze turned downward, more or less in line with the slope of your nose. In sessions to come, feel free to experiment with eyes open and eyes closed. Adjust your practice to the circumstances of each session or even to various stages in each session. Eyes closed reduces external visual distraction but may contribute to sleepiness and dulness. Eyes open may help to stay alert but may at first contribute to visual distraction and reduced focus. Some traditions recommend eyes open. It is a practice that quickly becomes comfortable.

The basic instruction for this first meditation is simply this: "Feel the body breathing and let go of everything else."

That is all you need to know and all you need to do. With this simple instruction you can go all the way to awakening. There is nothing else to do because the breathing is already happening, the sitting is already happening, and the physical sensations of sitting and breathing are already happening.

The rest of what follows is mostly clarification.

Notice where you can most readily begin to feel the physical sensations of breathing. That may be in different parts of the body in different meditation sessions, even at different times within the same mediation session. Just follow the cycles of

inhaling and exhaling as closely as you can.
Do so with ease and without trying to force
anything, either the breath itself or even your
attention. Practice this easy attention with
the same lightness with which a butterfly
lands on a flower. Practice what the Buddha
called bare attention: just feeling the
breathing, effortlessly and without naming
anything or adding anything to the physical
sensations.

Make sure your attention is on the
ever-changing breathing itself, not on you
doing the breathing, and not on you doing
the meditating. This is often an extremely
subtle issue but it is all-important. When
your attention is on the breathing itself you
are actually meditating. When your
attention is on you doing the breathing or
you doing the meditating or on the
meditation instructions you are merely

*thinking about yourself and about
meditating. This is almost the opposite of
meditating and a great hindrance to it.*

*Whenever you notice your mind
wandering to other things, which it will
because that is normal, simply let go and
return to feeling the physical experience of
breathing. Remember to check your posture
when your mind wanders—sitting with
dignity, with your back straight but not
straining—and become once again aware of
feeling the physical sensations of breathing.*

*A multitude of other things, both from
inside and outside, will appear in your
awareness and will clamor for your
attention. Notice them as they appear and let
them go, but without commenting or judging
or even naming them, and without becoming*

drawn in by them and letting your attention be carried away by them.

Always bring your attention back to the physical sensations of breathing, and let go of everything else that enters your mind. This is a practice of developing radically accepting awareness. The more often you have to let go of things and to bring your attention back the better. For that is the essence, the active ingredient, of this practice. Each time is a mini-awakening. With a few days of practice your ability to stay focused will start to improve. Aim to come as close as you can to hundred percent focus hundred percent of the time, but do not berate yourself for what actually happens. Rather, accept it as a mini-awakening.

There is nothing to do besides feeling the breathing. There is nowhere else to be but here, now. Let go of silently adding words or commentary or judgment. Let go of adding interpretation or analysis. Sit without expectations. Sit without preferences.

The entire session is aimed at doing as little as possible, and doing nothing at all is best of all. It is like watching a river of temporary experiences flowing by. Nothing to do but letting go, watching the river of experiences flow by.

This core meditation of just feeling the breathing and letting go of everything else is about refraining from getting carried away by doing all of the things our mind normally does in everyday life. It is aimed at letting go of getting lost in thinking. It is a practice of increasing bare attention and of reducing thinking.

When we practice this there is nothing to figure out. There is nothing to question and nothing to analyze. There is nothing to believe, nothing to understand, nothing to know, nothing to think about, nothing to worry about, nothing to resolve. There is nothing to do but feel the sensations of breathing and letting go of everything else.

There is nothing to look for and nothing to wait for. There is nothing we need to make happen in our awareness and nothing we need to prevent from happening. There is nothing to aim for and nothing to achieve. There is nothing to expect and nothing to wish for. There is nothing to hope for and nothing to strive for. There is only letting go of everything except feeling the physical sensations of breathing.

There is nothing to concentrate on, nothing to meditate on, and nothing to contemplate. There is nothing to reject and nothing to prefer. There is nothing to be disappointed by. There is only practicing bare attention to feeling the breathing and letting go of everything else.

There is nothing to succeed in and nothing to fail at. There is nothing to do right and nothing to do wrong. There is nothing to compare. There is nothing that is better and nothing that is worse.

As you can see, this core meditation is not at all about doing something special or doing something esoteric or difficult. It is precisely about not doing anything at all. The more you practice this the more any unhappiness of the moment begins to melt and dissolve. It eventually begins to be replaced by a felt sense of deep contentment, peace, and lightheartedness. For as you will learn over time, in your own direct experience, unhappiness cannot arise when your attention is on here, now, this, without adding commentary.

The more you practice this core meditation the more you become aware of habitual thoughts and beliefs about yourself that are monkey traps and that create your many familiar experiences of private unhappiness. Practicing just feeling the physical sensations of breathing with bare attention and letting go of everything else is a practice of willing suspension of all beliefs about yourself. It is about learning to let go so you are not caught in self-made monkey traps.

3

Where is your unhappiness? The unfindable personal self

View

We learn how to be unhappy without needing a teacher for it. We spontaneously create our individual ways of being unhappy. We are perhaps nowhere more inventive and unique than in this area of our life. Our unhappiness may well be our most original personal achievement. First we invent it and then we rehearse and repeat it again and again. We do this by responding to many new situations we encounter according to old and fixed habit patterns. We automatically lapse into familiar states whenever the conditions are right for it, or even when they merely remind us of previous experiences of unhappiness. As others have said, we are always practicing something, and for many of us it is our unhappiness we practice most.

Philosophers have recognized that being unhappy is not only an occasional and situational thing. It is not merely a sort of aberration that takes us off course. It is an essential part of what it means to be human. None of us lives in paradise. Whatever paradise we may imagine belongs in some long ago past that is no more, or in some even more distant past that may never have been.

We often blame circumstances and events for this lack of bliss. But in the end we secretly blame ourselves most of all. We have invented the notion that we must somehow be marked by a profound inadequacy. Some have called it "original sin." We are convinced of having an inborn quality of not being good enough. We believe that we are not deserving of lasting happiness, that we are not fit for it. Yes, we may experience times of pleasure, but reliably lasting happiness eludes us. We are convinced that it is beyond our reach.

In all the endless variations on this theme there is the core idea of a fundamental and built-in deficiency. We imagine this imperfection at the heart of our individual person, but we also project it on the world around us. We may then see it as part of the culture in which we grew up and live. Or we may see it at the heart of human nature and of the human condition itself. Adam and Eve simply had to be expelled from paradise in our imagination. We have no other explanation for our normal existential unhappiness than the belief that we humans are simply not paradise material. And so, as the story of that biblical expulsion says, we must endlessly toil. But even that does not get us back to paradise. Nirvana seems out of reach. It must be otherworldly. And so we have a vast and drama-filled literature around the theme of Paradise Lost. And as an indication of just how endless our struggle with this idea has been, we also have a host of philosophies, religions, theologies, psychologies, and sociologies around the theme, the hope, or the promise of some form of Paradise Regained.

We do not have to believe in original sin to know that we have a unique capacity to be unhappy even in the best of circumstances. In our heart of hearts each of us also seems to believe that nobody does unhappiness better than we do unhappiness. We almost pride ourselves in the uniqueness of our personal unhappiness. This is so much the case that we won't let anyone talk us out it. As Freud observed, our unhappiness is the last thing we will let anyone take away from us.

When we live long enough and if we can be honest with ourselves we recognize that our life is in important ways not going where we would like it to go. To be sure, we may have achieved certain successes and we may have experienced certain pleasures. But even when that is the case something remains unsatisfied deep down. When this begins to bother us enough, and eventually too much, we can go into psychotherapy to see if that can rescue us. But psychotherapy has had little to show for itself in making us a happier species. It can at best turn neurotic misery into normal complaints, but without doing anything about natural unhappiness.

But there *is* something we *can* do. We do not have to let a psychotherapist tell us the story of our unhappiness—in the way that Peter Quince tells Bottom the story of his bewildering experiences in Shakespeare's play. We can go to work on reclaiming our birthright to a natural and inborn experience of lightheartedness. Freud, the founding father of modern psychotherapy, considered himself an archaeologist of the soul. In meditational self-care we become a psychological researcher in our own right, albeit not an archaeologist. We become the researcher of our unhappiness by asking one question: "Where is it?"

This one question—"Where is it?"—is the most penetrating meditational research method into our life. It functions as a searchlight with which we investigate every nook and cranny of our experiences. We look everywhere to see if we can find where our unhappiness is located. We thereby end up looking for what we consider our personal self. But when we search deeply we discover that this personal self is unfindable. That discovery makes all the difference. It is what begins to set us free from our private or innermost unhappiness.

Asking "Where is our unhappy self?" is not a mind game. It is not an intellectual game. And it is not a word game. It is not handled with words, and it is not answered with words. It is a wordless inquiry on which the quality of our life and of our future depends. It examines the imagined existence and the essential nature of the unhappy self.

In everyday life we act as if the unhappy self were a definable person. We believe it is an independently existing being with a more or less fixed identity. The idea of the unhappy personal self is a variation on the theme of a fixed original sin. Except that we do not just believe that we *have* an unhappy personal self. We think we *are* it. And we think we *are* it because we talk ourselves into believing that it is what makes us real.

Meditational self-care leads us to a liberating view and a felt experience that are at first perplexing and difficult to grasp. It says: Don't be resentful and ungrateful for your unhappiness. It says: Don't reject it, because it is precisely your unhappiness that can help you see the very things that make being human priceless. For meditational self-care replaces private unhappiness with a deeply felt affirmation of existence.

With meditational self-care we become grateful to our personal unhappiness. For paradoxically, when we handle personal unhappiness with meditational self-care we learn to transcend it and to set ourselves free. We discover a way to exist in a mode of contentment and lightheartedness—no matter what has happened, no matter what is happening, and no matter what is going to happen. This includes not only all our sorrows, disappointments, and losses but also our aging process, our eventual illness, and our certain death.

The practice of searching to find our unhappy self involves looking through all our familiar experiences. That includes all our gross and subtle physical sensations, all our pleasant and unpleasant feelings, all our thoughts, and all our habitual emotional and behavioral response patterns. We discover that we cannot find this unhappy self, even though it has always seemed so clear and so real, and even though it has always felt so close as to make us believe it is who we are.

It is precisely through the process of searching for a personal self that we discover it to be unfindable. We cannot put our finger on it. We cannot point to it. We cannot capture it in an identifying definition. We cannot discover it as a more or less solid entity, a thing-in-itself. This does not mean that our experiences are unreal, or that the world is unreal, or that our personal unhappiness is unreal. It means that they cannot be pinpointed as solid things. They cannot be found as any kind of thing-in-itself. It also means that we do not have to remain stuck to our unhappiness as a monkey is stuck in its trap. Our unhappiness can be removed by being dissolved, and it can be dissolved by letting go of our belief in it as a solid fact. It is not an indelible stain, an "original sin." It is not an inherent and incurable deficiency.

But what remains, then, when we discover that we cannot find a fixed, solid, personal self? What remains is awareness itself. What remains is awareness that experiences everything and that knows all experiences but that does not close its fist around any of them and becomes stuck to them. What remains is an all-embracing awareness that experiences everything but that is itself, like a mirror, unaffected and unchanged by anything that appears in it. It is like space, which contains all things but which is itself without limit and which cannot be contained by anything. This is how events and experiences lose their impact: by losing their grip on us. They lose their ability to leave an imprint, in the same way that images fail to leave an imprint on the mirror in which they appear. This is how our monkey mind frees itself from its trap.

Much of this is difficult to understand at first. It may seem too nonsensical and too fantastic to be true. It is something we must experience personally and directly before we can realize it. We cannot know it with words or verbally based thinking. Words only serve as suggestions. They point us in a certain direction so that we may look in that direction and come to see for ourselves what is being pointed out.

A true understanding of what is at stake only comes from the practice and the direct experience of engaging in meditational self-care. Remember that meditational self-care is not an intellectual activity, a theory, a doctrine, or a body of ideas or information. It is not something to think or talk about. It is something to do and to experience in the doing. Hence the practices it suggests.

Practice

The instruction for this meditation is simple. It is to learn the habit of asking one question: "Where is it?"

The "it" here is twofold. It includes the personal self as well as all the thoughts, feelings, worries, and problems that are its usual and familiar concerns. You learn to ask this one question, "Where is it?", until you discover that you cannot locate either the personal self or any of its concerns. All that remains is awareness itself, awareness that is everywhere but that cannot be pointed at.

Begin by evoking a felt sense of what it is like to be you. That includes the general and familiar sense of being who you are, plus perhaps the emotional state that is coloring this usual and familiar sense of who you are at this moment. Then focus on feeling the physical sensations in the body as they appear in awareness, but without getting caught up in words and concepts, and ask, "Where is the personal self?"

You don't have to do anything special for this. Just be aware of any and all physical sensations you experience, and see whether you can find a solid self among them. There may be physical sensations of barely perceptible tingling, or muscle tension, or sensations of energy waves or energy pulses, or sensations of firmness or softness, or of warmth or coolness, or tension or relaxation, or any other physical sensations of which you become aware.

Slowly scan the total field of bodily sensations, from the bottom of your feet to the top of your head. See if you can let yourself consciously feel all the physical sensations you notice, but without silently involving the usual name or the concept of familiar body parts. Feel the sensations just as they appear in awareness, but without referring to hand, leg, chest, back, head, or other body parts. These words and names of body parts are concepts. They are not direct physical sensations. You don't feel your hand or leg, only the physical sensations in what you call your hand or leg. In order to see this clearly and directly look as closely as you can at the precise physical sensations you feel. If you look close the usual concepts and names fall away and dissolve. Only the direct and precise experience remains. If you think you nonetheless come upon some solid, firm, or fixed entity of any kind, look even closer at the physical sensation until the newly found entity dissolves and disappears altogether. With practice you become better at just experiencing physical sensations without

referring with words to added-on concepts
and names of body parts. Over time you may
notice that even the very concept of the body
as a whole begins to fade, dissolve, and fall
away altogether. And with the disappearing
sense of a body with fixed and solid parts you
may discover that the very experience of a
personal self as a firm and fixed entity begins
to dissolve as well. It begins to fade and fall
away altogether. All that remains are
discrete physical sensations (and later also
discrete mental contents).

No matter where you search and look
in the body as a concept you will discover
that you cannot find a solid personal self.
There is no findable solid self anywhere you
look.

In similar fashion, when you broaden
your awareness beyond physical sensations
and when you open up to all other
experiences that arise in awareness you will

notice that they too, like the physical sensations, are not bound up with any fixed entity such as your assumed and body-based identity. Any thoughts, feelings, emotional impulses, words, phrases, or reaction patterns that appear in awareness, any images, fragments of day dreams, memories, or anything else—all this appears as momentary or transient experiences that arise spontaneously. They linger for a while, briefly or longer as the case may be, and then they disappear without involving any identifiable and fixed entity like a personal self. Unifying experiences like the sense of being or of having a personal self, or a personal body, are ideas of the intellect, not direct experiences.

What remains, then, when there is no personal self to be found? What remains is subtler but larger than any familiar or imaginable personal self or than any temporary experience. For what remains is awareness itself. It contains everything that appears in it but it cannot itself be contained or even pointed at. What remains is the ever-present capacity and process of being aware—effortlessly, and independent of a personal self.

Awareness contains everything that appears in it, just like a mirror. Like a mirror it is none of the things it contains and of which you become aware. And like a mirror it is not affected or changed by any experience that appears in it.

Awareness is not a solid thing, like the imagined solid body or the imagined personal self. It is neither a definable thing-in-itself nor something personal that one can point at and consider personal property. Here the notion of what we usually call "me" or "mine" or "I" dissolves. Yet all experiences remain the same, as real as ever. Nothing is changed or denied, and nothing is taken away from your life. All that is dissolved is the belief in a solid self, the belief in a self that is defined by the concept of body and that thinks itself to be the owner of all that it experiences.

We are not who we think we are. For the sake of the mundane concerns and the practicalities of everyday life it is necessary to assume the feeling and the usual sense of having or of being our familiar personal identity. But, contrary to the beliefs of everyday life, that is not who we really are at a more fundamental level. Who or what we really are is awareness itself, which is larger than anything and everything it contains.

Nothing changes when this begins to dawn, except that the heavy burden of it all being a weight on our shoulders and in our heart begins to be lifted. We become the opposite of Atlas carrying the weight of the

*universe on his shoulders. A feeling of
lightheartedness and of the onset of
contentment and peace begins to replace the
heaviness of our familiar burdens and of our
personal unhappiness.*

*Over time and as your meditation
practice becomes more flexible you can and
you need to do this practice with every
experience, with every internal or external
event. You can do it with every feeling of
familiar unhappiness, every unhappy-
making thought and belief, every inherited or
learned idea that can weigh down your mind
and your feelings about your life. With all of
these you ask: Where is it?*

*But you can and you must also do it
with every cherished happiness or with every
happy-making thought, for they are not solid
facts either, only temporary appearances in
awareness. Clinging to happy thoughts,
feelings, and experiences is a subtle and*

seductive but deeply unhelpful way to remain
attached to the notion of a personal self.

Look at everything, absolutely
everything, that appears in your experience
in the same way and ask the same question:
Where is it? Look for how it manifests itself,
of what particular experiences it consists,
and where it may seem to be located in your
body and where it seems to make itself felt.
Look closely until you realize that you cannot
find it because it is nowhere but in awareness
itself. Then rest and continue to dwell in
what is left: awareness itself, awareness that
is aware of everything yet not burdened and
weighed down by any of it. Linger and dwell
on this until you begin to develop a growing
sense of awareness itself, until you can begin
to see that you are awareness itself.

By beginning to let go of the sense of a
solid personal self and of every seemingly
solid event, experience, fact, or thing you

begin to liberate yourself from clinging to your private unhappiness, and from being trapped and imprisoned by it. It dissolves the mind-made and learned private unhappiness that arises from believing who you think you are. This is what is meant by "awakening to awareness itself." It is an awakening from the dream of having and being a personal self.

4

Open wide—to awareness itself, which is as vast as space

View

"Awareness" may be a better term to speak about our experience of being alive and conscious than "the mind." In everyday life it is convenient to speak about "the mind" as if it were a kind of nonphysical but nonetheless organ-like entity, something that is associated with the brain. But between what we know as the physical brain and what we mean by the notion of a nonphysical mind there exists an unbridgeable gap. It is the same unbridgeable gap that exists between a carved wooden puppet that looks like a boy and a living and conscious human being named Pinocchio.

Brain science can easily become a variation on the Pinocchio fantasy. It too can give rise to the belief that a cleverly made mechanical model may one day become equal to a living and conscious human. But nothing we can ever say about brain models or the mind as a mechanism can tell us what living experience and consciousness are. Speaking about "awareness" instead of "the mind" helps to protect us against believing the Pinocchio fantasy.

We usually and naturally speak about "*the* mind." In contrast, most of the time we naturally say "awareness," not "the awareness." "Awareness" without "the" in front of it suggests something more elusive than a thing we can point at. "Awareness" suggests something less circumscribed, less limited, less easily definable, and less capable of being pointed at as if it were an object that we can locate and manipulate.

Awareness is more like space than it is like any particular thing in space. Space is boundless, while particular things in it are not. Awareness is similarly boundless. Space cannot be pointed at, even though it is everywhere. Awareness is similarly incapable of being pointed at, even though it is everywhere the ground of all experience. Just as space is what makes it possible for things to be in it, so too is boundless awareness what makes it possible for bounded experiences to be at all. But at the same time, just as space becomes meaningful only because there are things in it, so too is awareness meaningful only because of the experiences that appear in it. Awareness cannot be separated from the experiences that appear in it—anymore than a mirror can exist by itself without reflecting anything.

There are two levels of knowing. The first focuses on content, the second on what contains all content. The first is about specific experiences, the second is about what does the experiencing. Meditational self-care is aimed at shifting the basis from which we function to the boundless vastness of awareness itself—but without losing sight of anything that appears in it. Meditational self-care shifts us from a historically conditioned and reactive personal sense of self to an open, space-like awareness that is nonreactive, like a mirror. This level of knowing is no longer personal and bound to historical events or circumstances. The meditation tradition calls this shift in the level of knowing "awakening to awareness itself."

We love to look at the vast night sky, at the boundless space, and at the innumerable stars in it. These resonate with an equivalent vastness, boundlessness, and richness inside our hearts and minds. That is the reason why philosophers through the ages have said that the depth of the soul is unfathomable, and that its limits cannot be found because there are no limits to it. Meditational self-care turns this intellectual idea into a direct experience. It does so with practices that are aimed at developing a felt sense of awareness itself.

During the day we can easily see all the things around us and when we look up at the sky we may see clouds or the blueness of the sky. But even when we look up at the sky during the day we do not see the vastness of space. That is why we love a clear night sky. It lets us see the vastness of space. What moves us so deeply in a clear night sky is that we know ourselves to be within that boundless space. We know ourselves to be part of it. We know that it is this vast space that lets us be here. Even our seemingly solid body, our seemingly solid person, is itself part of space and made possible by it. Awareness itself is like that. It is like the all-encompassing, all-embracing, boundless, and ever-present vastness of space.

Making the shift from a reactive personal self to a nonreactive sense of awareness itself involves developing what the meditation tradition calls a "lion's gaze." When you throw a stick in front of a dog the dog chases after the stick. In contrast, when you throw a stick in front of a lion the lion gazes at the source of the stick but without running after the stick itself. Similarly, the personal self is naturally compelled to chase after everything that enters the mind. Awakening to awareness itself is like learning to watch the source from which everything arises but without reactively chasing after everything that does arise.

Nothing changes in our life with this shift in our level of knowing, this shift of awakening to awareness itself. And yet everything becomes different. Nothing is lost and everything remains as before. But now it exists as if in a breeze of lightheartedness that is free from personal unhappiness. We thereby gain our freedom from habits of thinking that first create our distress out of the belief in a personal self, and that then keep us imprisoned in our monkey traps because we cling to that belief.

The image or metaphor of vast, boundless space, like that of a nonreactive mirror, is one of the traditional ways to speak about awareness itself. There have been other images and metaphors that are meant to do the same thing, and we will take a look at them here. Collectively these images and metaphors serve as pointers. They help us look in the right direction and in the right way, so that we may come to see what awareness itself is about. But these images and metaphors themselves are not awareness itself. Nor are they any kind of final and definitive statement about awareness itself. A finger pointing to the moon is not the moon itself. Similarly, the images and metaphors that are used to point to awareness itself are not awareness itself. Getting caught up in "believing" those images or metaphors and clinging to them as if they were a new and definitive truth is simply another way of missing the sense of awareness itself in favor of chasing after a new stick that appears in it.

It is nonetheless worth dwelling on those images and metaphors that have been used to point to awareness itself. Just as we may sit down to look with rapt interest through a box of pictures or an art book, so too can we look closely at these images and metaphors. When we do this with fully absorbed attention we can begin to develop a more directly and more deeply felt sense of what they reveal. That way they stop being mere intellectual ideas and they become directly experienced realities.

When we think of awareness as being like space it becomes easier to see that it contains everything possible and imaginable. There is no event so big and no experience so overwhelming, even if it seems to take up every square inch of our life and of our mind, that is not itself contained by awareness as if by space. Looking at all experiences this way, with a felt sense for the space in which they arise, creates a feeling of relief and of having more room to breathe and to maneuver. It sets in motion our liberation from a claustrophobic view of our experiences and our life. It opens the felt sense of our life to the size of infinite space. Doing meditational self-care amounts to becoming like a space gazer. It means always looking to see and to sense the vast, the all-encompassing, the endless space of awareness itself that contains all our individual experiences. The felt sense and the belief of having or being a small personal self begin to dissolve. They are replaced by a felt sense of being like something that is insubstantial but real, infinitely larger, and endlessly less burdensome than an individual identity.

The metaphor of a mirror adds an important feature to our understanding of awareness itself. Likening awareness to a mirror points to the ability to reflect and contain everything we experience but without triggering our usual reactivity. For awareness itself, just like a mirror, is unaffected and unchanged by what appears in it. When we are like a mirror everything we encounter and experience continues to appear just as before. But now it does so without setting off the habitual defensiveness of our imagined and eternally threatened personal self.

Awareness itself can also be likened to a world of perpetual stillness. It is like an ever-present stillness that contains and provides room for all the activities, events, happenings, emotions, commotions, habits, and thinking that shape the drama of our life. While these give rise to a sense of perpetual motion, awareness itself remains as the basis and the boundless realm of stillness that encompasses all motion and all anxious restlessness. It remains as a boundless universe that is never anything but still, even when everything in it seems to be in a state of perpetual and unstoppable unrest.

Awareness itself has also been likened to a vast and ever-present world of silence. As a vast and ever-present silence awareness itself provides room for all the sound and fury of the world's clamoring. It is a silence that contains and holds our endless and reactive commentary on everything. This silence remains present beneath and in the midst of all clamoring sound and fury. It is not destroyed or displaced and made to disappear by sound and by fury. Rather, awareness itself is like the supporting silence in which all sound appears. It is the necessary ground of silence that makes all sound possible. It is the invisible and intangible foundation without which it would be impossible for there to be any sound at all.

Awareness itself has also been likened to the vastness of the world ocean. This world ocean is always simultaneously changing and unchanging. Like this world ocean awareness itself is eternal yet constantly producing endless waves of temporary experiences. Like waves these experiences rise and fall. They roll in and they pass by. Like an ocean awareness itself remains undisturbed by its own perpetual waves. It lets them arise and roll by without itself being changed.

Developing a felt sense of awareness itself begins by asking "Where is it?" in response to every experience that arises. This is not an inquiry into a place. It is a searching for the vastness of space that makes all places possible and that contains all places, as well as all things, all events, and all experiences.

But awakening to awareness itself is more than merely thinking or arguing about an idea, a theory, or a belief. It is not the pursuit of an idea, a theory, or a belief. It is not a question of grasping and tightly holding on to one more idea, theory, or belief. It must not become a new way of getting caught in images and metaphors, like a monkey in a trap. It is a practice of seeing certain helpful images and metaphors as pointers that point beyond themselves. It is done in order to develop immediate or "unmediated" knowledge of what is being pointed to when we think and talk about awareness itself and awakening to it.

This direct knowing is more of a revelatory nature than of an informational or intellectual nature. We can set the conditions for this revelatory knowing to happen, but we cannot force it happen. Yet while none of us can make it happen, all of us have the inborn and natural ability to experience it happening. With meditational self-care, as with the meditation tradition, we can create the conditions.

With our practice we set the conditions to discover for ourselves that all experience of reality exists in awareness, that it depends on awareness, and that there is in the end nothing but awareness to experience. We set the conditions to discover firsthand and with a clear vision that reality *is* awareness, and that awareness *is* reality.

Why does all this matter? It matters for the following reason. As a contemporary teacher of these things put it, when you lose touch with the felt sense of inner space, stillness, and silence you lose touch with your essential nature, which is awareness itself. And when you lose touch with your essential nature of awareness itself you lose yourself in the dramas of your life and the world.

More positively stated, and as another teacher put it, awakening to awareness itself makes us see that there are two kinds of dreams: the short ones and the long one. The short ones we dream at night. The long one is our everyday life.

Practice

This is a practice you start with your eyes open.

Look at something right in front of you and ask, "Where is it?" Your natural inclination is to say, "Right there." But then ask, "Where is there?" More precisely, ask, "Where is the thereness of the thing you are looking at? How do you know it is there?" If you answer: "I know it because I see it," ask again: "Where is the seeing? Where is the knowing?" Press hard with these questions. Do not answer them with ready-made intellectual beliefs and with the kind of thinking that comes out of already-knowing. Handle the questions not by rummaging through ideas you have had for a long time. Handle them instead by personally searching in your immediate and fresh experience.

When you press hard you discover something that begins to change everything. You discover that without the seeing, without the knowing you cannot experience that there is something to see and to know. The seeing, the knowing, the experiencing are your reality. Press hard until you can see for yourself, from your immediate and fresh experience, that "thereness" is something that awareness lets you see, and know, and experience. Look and search until you can see that "thereness" is in awareness and nowhere else. This same searching inquiry can be applied to all the realities you can possibly experience, every single one of them.

The total reality of all that we ever experience can be grouped into familiar clusters. These include the body, other people, thoughts, feelings and impulses of every kind, all that has happened in what we call our history, and even the very notion of history and time itself. The remainder of this session is devoted to searching each of these familiar clusters of experiences. Always we shine light and generate insight by asking the same question, "Where is it?"

The first cluster of experiences to search in this way is the body. It is natural to identify our sense of being who are with our experience of the body. It would be unnatural and impractical if we did not have this starting point. But even though this is perfectly appropriate for everyday living, things are different at the level of more ultimate realities.

As you are sitting, ask yourself: "Where are your hands?" It seems obvious where they are. You can see them right there, or feel them, or picture them. But as before ask: "Where is that feeling, that seeing, that knowing? Where is that right-thereness?" Search diligently, as if for the first time.

Search until your knowledge of the answer becomes free from already-knowing or preconception. Search until you can clearly see that your hands are in awareness itself. There would be no hands to see, feel, or picture without awareness. Make sure that this is clear, as a directly felt discovery, not merely as a new thinking habit that you are developing as a result of doing this practice.

Then, if you wish, you can go on like this through your entire body. You can go through the entire field of all the separate parts that make up your knowledge and understanding of what your body is. Picture every part until you have a convincing and directly felt sense that your entire body is in awareness. There would be no body to have, to know, to experience, or even to study without awareness. Keep searching until you discover for yourself that you are not in the

first place a free-standing thing-in-itself
called a body. You are in the first place
awareness—awareness that cannot be
located anywhere but that contains
everything, including every part of your
body and even the very idea of a body.

Now close your eyes and do the same
thing with the next cluster of familiar
experiences, what we normally think of as
"everybody else." In dealing with other
people we naturally think of them as "they"
or "them." They are part of the seeming "out-
thereness" of the world. But here as well ask:
"Where are they?" Again you are to search
not by rummaging through all the things you
already know in your preconceptions. You
are to search by asking: "Where is that
thereness of other people?" Search as if this
were your first search ever.

The purpose here is not to deny the reality of other people. And it is not to deny the reality of your experience of them. It is to clarify your understanding of the relation between awareness and reality. The nature of that relation has been obscured by your personal development and history. This has included learning false ideas. First among these false ideas is the fundamental duality of "me" and "not-me" from which all other dualities arise. Asking, "Where is everybody else?" helps to remove what obscures the true nature of the relation between awareness and reality. It dismantles erroneous ideas and beliefs about dualities. It thereby contributes to dismantling the mind-made unhappiness that grows out of living a life built around false dualities.

As you cross paths with other people in your life, or as they cross your mind when

you think about them, ask the same question:
"Where are they?" The first, reflexive, and
conditioned response is naturally dualistic:
"They are not here, where I am, but there,
where I am not and where I can see them or
where I imagine them as I think about them."
The overlearned habit and the strong pull of
thinking in terms of "out-thereness" make
you expect that other people are "out there,"
and that this is a place where you are not,
because you are in a place you call "here."
But there is only one place where they can
be: in awareness. It is only there, in
awareness, that you experience them. Your
awareness of other people is all you know of
them. They are not only in awareness itself.
They are made possible by awareness itself.
There would be no other people in your life
without your awareness of them.

This practice makes you begin to look at other people and at your experience of them with a fresh attitude. It changes how you walk through the world and how you experience it. It begins to make you more tolerant, more patient, more compassionate, and kinder—with others, and also with yourself. It makes you see that how we feel and think about other people does not depend on them but on us.

The next application of this practice addresses the cluster of experiences that we think of as being "in here"—the inner world of thoughts, feelings, memories, mental images, and impulses. It is easy and natural to think of "in here" in a manner that is analogous to thinking about "out there." But just as with everything that seems to be "out there," ask, "Where are your thoughts, your

feelings, your memories, your mental
images, your impulses?"

Bring to mind a familiar thought,
feeling, memory, mental image, or impulse
that often intrudes in your awareness.
Perhaps something that comes to you
automatically, something you cannot seem to
shake off when it appears, no matter how
hard you try. Ask: "Where is that thought or
that feeling, memory, mental image, or
impulse?" Inquire deeply and ask: "Where is
it before it arises?" and "Where does it go
when you stop thinking, feeling, seeing, or
sensing it?" "Where is it when you are
experiencing it?" Look closely until you see
that the thought, the feeling, the memory, the
mental image, or the impulse appears in
awareness, but that you cannot say where,
or how it arises, or where it goes when it
goes away.

If you believe, based on accepted knowledge, that these things are in your head, in your brain, look more closely at your actual experience. Where in your head can you sense them and find them? Where are they in your immediate experience of them? Look closely until you can clearly see that even the very idea of "head" or "brain" is itself a thought, simply another thought, another thought that exists in awareness and nowhere else. There would be no notion of "head" or "brain" without awareness.

There would be no brain science were it not for awareness. In the end all brain science is about itself alone, about brain science, before it is about any such thing-in-itself as a "brain" that exists independent of the notion of "brain," which is a thought, not a thing. As you can see, meditational self-

care is personally conducted awareness science. It is an experiential science in which only what you discover for yourself counts for anything. It is not brain science that is conducted by others whom you must believe because they have credentials which you may not have.

We now turn the same method of inquiry to the habit of describing our experiences in terms of the history of what has happened in our life. We are the protagonist of the drama of our life that we tell ourselves and others. Western psychology has long regarded personal dramatic history as the best way to describe and to account for a human life. The belief is that telling the story of the events of our life is the same thing as telling the truth about that life. Now the time has come to ask: "Where is that story that defines you?"

*More precisely, "Where are the events
and the experiences of your history?" And
beyond that, "Where is history itself?" Look
directly, without mediation by familiar
thoughts and long-held beliefs. Look until
you can see that all the things you know
about yourself exist not "out there" or "in
here" but in awareness itself. They exist as a
story you are telling yourself and others.
This life as you have lived it, as you are
currently living it, and as you will go on
living it—this life has been taking place, is
taking place, and will continue to take place
in awareness itself, and nowhere else. You
live in awareness more than you live in the
physical place that is your address or in your
social and historical circumstance. You live
in the present of awareness, the ever-present
present of awareness.*

In the rest of this session or in future sessions you can practice this inquiry with all the major historical episodes and events of your life, and with all the figures in them. Do so until you realize, directly and convincingly, that your history is in your ever-present awareness and nowhere else. Practice this until you have a clear sense that you are more a product of awareness than you are a product of your alleged history or of anything you can name in that alleged history.

The last application of the searching question of "Where?" concerns the very notion of time itself. Ask, "Where is the past?" and "Where is the future?" You find that all there is, is awareness itself, which is always now. But awareness is not the present as one of three time zones, the one that is squeezed between what came before and what comes next. It is the ever-ongoing process of being present, of witnessing the experiences that appear in awareness. Now is nothing less than the vast and boundless space of awareness—the vast stillness and silence of awareness, the mirror that witnesses everything, the unchanging ocean that is full of its own ever-changing and temporary waves rolling by.

With these repeated searches you are familiarizing yourself with the practice of sensing that there is always a space around everything you experience. There is always a stillness, a silence, an ocean, or a mirror. Absolutely everything you experience is contained by something that is larger than it, even though it cannot be seen or pointed at.

That sense of space is normally absent from our everyday experiences. These seem

*to take up every inch of our life. There often
seems to be no room to spare, no room to
maneuver, and no room to breathe. In our
habitual ways we become totally identified
with our experiences of the moment. They
seem to shape every aspect of the sense of
who we are. The practice of seeing that
everything we experience is contained in
boundless awareness begins to liberate us
from the oppressive and claustrophobic sense
of complete identification with our
experiences of the moment.*

*Now finish this session by going back
to the core practice of just sitting and
breathing. Start by becoming aware of the
physical sensations of just sitting and
breathing. After a few minutes of this, open
up to everything of which you become aware,
without focusing on anything in particular.
Let yourself become aware not only of*

physical sensations but also of sounds and smells and of images, thoughts, impulses, feelings, memory flashes—anything that enters into awareness.

But now, instead of focusing your attention on all this content that appears in awareness, see if you can develop a felt sense of awareness itself. See if you can develop a sense of the silent stillness in which all of it is appearing. See if you can develop a sense of the mirror-like receptivity of awareness that accepts everything and that judges, rejects, or reacts to nothing. See if you can develop a felt sense of the boundless spaciousness of awareness itself, of the ocean of awareness that is full of the endless coming and going of ever-changing waves of experiences.

See if you can let these images and metaphors of space, silence, stillness, mirror, and ocean become felt experiences. Take a few moments or minutes to dwell in the felt sense of space, silence, stillness, mirror, and ocean, without doing anything else. Take a few moments or minutes to let yourself be the space, be the silence, be the stillness, be the mirror, be the ocean. For that is your true nature. That is who you are.

And whenever you get a chance in your everyday life, listen to silence when you hear it, and feel stillness when you sense it. Practicing this "externally" promotes your ability to do so "internally."

5

Don't believe *anything* you think: Be like a mirror

View

Western therapeutic psychology says, "Don't believe everything you think." What we think shapes how we feel about ourselves, our life, and the world. Much of what we think about ourselves, our life, and the world is not true. It is therefore unwise to automatically believe everything we think.

Depressed people are a good example. They believe many things about themselves, their life, and the world that are negative and pessimistic—but often also untrue. They think themselves into depressed states. They do not just get caught in mind-made monkey traps. They spin complete cocoons of untrue negative beliefs and then they live in those cocoons. They close themselves off from a life that can be richer than what they imagine and believe. They do the opposite of opening up to awareness itself. The result is emotional contraction, constriction, diminishment, and impoverishment.

Psychological treatment of depression involves three steps. First comes learning to recognize self-defining beliefs that contribute to depressed states. Then comes challenging those beliefs to see if they are true or false. The third step is letting go of false beliefs and replacing them with true and life promoting thoughts. This is a slow and tedious process. It takes time, patience, and endless repetition. It requires more than unmasking specific beliefs that are depressing but false. It must include undoing the very habit of obsessively and compulsively thinking depressing thoughts. Hence the principle of, "Don't believe everything you think."

The meditation tradition has been teaching the same principle for thousands of years, but it has from the beginning gone a giant step further. It does not just say: "Don't believe everything you think." That is only half of the wisdom needed to free ourselves from mind-made unhappiness. The counsel of, "Don't believe everything you think," is a good start but an incomplete strategy.

Completing this half-wisdom is done by the more radical meditational approach that says: "Don't believe *anything* you think." It is difficult to overestimate just how radical this is and how far its implications reach. But again, this is not something to be understood merely intellectually. It is not something to be argued intellectually. It is something to be discovered personally and experientially.

The counsel of, "Don't believe everything you think," may help to dissolve specific unhappy-making beliefs but it keeps the notion of the personal self intact. It merely spruces up the personal self-image. This may yield certain limited benefits, to be sure, but it maintains the fundamental identification with the personal self as the basis of all experience.

It is only the suspension of *all* beliefs and of the very activity of believing, not just the suspension of some beliefs, that shifts us out of being identified with an imagined personal self. Only that way can we move to a liberated position in awareness itself. As already seen in previous views and practices, this involves learning to feel that we are, in our deepest nature, like space—or like stillness, silence, a mirror, or an ocean.

The great discovery of the meditation tradition is a paradox. It is the paradox that even though we usually do not realize it, in our deepest nature we always already are like space—or stillness, silence, a mirror, or an ocean. We do not have to make ourselves that way. We do not have to change first before things can become that way. We already are that way, from the start and at all times. We are that way in every moment, from moment to moment. We have learned to forget that this is how things are. We have learned to become preoccupied and busy with fending for the personal self. We have first created the belief in a personal self. Then we have come to depend on it and to defend it. And finally we have come to live for it and to do most of what we do for its sake.

The meditation tradition has cast the principle of, "Don't believe *anything* you think," in positive terms as well as negative terms. It has cast it in the form of a traditional instruction that says: "Walk as an illusory being in a dream." That does not mean that our experiences are unreal or that the world is unreal. It means that our usual feeling of having or of being a personal self, and of being surrounded by other solid selves, is like a dream from which we can awaken.

Psychologists speak of something they call "reification." That means, "real-making." It refers to the mental activity of treating as real something that is not. It makes the thing seem real so that it is experienced as real and believed to be real. It places the thing and the belief in it beyond question in its assumed reality. But as Nietzsche put it: "Facts are precisely what there are not, only interpretations." The most famous opening line from Western philosophy puts it this way: "The world is my representation." Transposed to the language of the meditation tradition that becomes: "The world is my awareness." The Buddha likened his discovery of this view to the experience of awakening from a dream.

If reification of the personal self and its worldview is what creates the mental prison of unhappiness, then dereification is the way to escape from it. We practice dereification by "walking as an illusory being in a dream." That means living with a clear and directly felt sense—not just the intellectual idea—that what we experience are not hard facts. What we experience at every moment are images that are created and experienced by awareness itself. Our personal self-images are like pictures projected on a screen by awareness itself. Recognizing this is like waking up from a dream of illusory realities. It means realizing that what we have been calling living has been a process of dreaming. It has been a process of unknowingly walking and acting as if in a dream.

The purpose of this practice is to counter the habit of creating mind-made unhappiness by what we think about ourselves. Since the guiding idea in meditational self-care is that we suffer from who we think we are, the remedy, to repeat, is to address this very issue. We do this with the practice of willing suspension of all beliefs. There are many ways to do this, but the active ingredient in the remedy is the same in each.

The meditation tradition has imagined a mythic figure who represents the practice of willing suspension of all beliefs. It has imagined a figure named Manjushri, who is holding a flaming sword. He personifies the Buddha's essential wisdom that cuts through all illusions and delusions. Manjushri's flaming sword is no ordinary sword for doing battle. It is a sword from whose flames spring the light of insight and the lightheartedness of awakening to awareness itself. The touch of his sword turns everything into an occasion of waking up and realizing the imagined and dream-like nature of all things and all beliefs. With its touch it lights up the realization that all experience and all reality appear in awareness itself, and as a manifestation of awareness itself.

Manjushri's sword is mythic, but it is neither mystical, nor mysterious, nor magical.

Understanding what it means does not require belief in mysticism, mystery, or magic. And it is not about practicing ritualistic behavior or putting on esoteric airs and mannerisms. It is utterly down to earth. It is as down-to-earth as the loving touch of a mother who comforts a child with soothing caresses and kisses. It is as powerful in its impact as the gesture of a parent or elder who, with the touch of a hand on a shoulder, bestows the blessing of goodwill and support on a younger generation. It is as dignifying as the gesture of a king who elevates a commoner to knighthood by tapping his shoulder with the royal sword. In each case there is a profoundly felt transformation. It is brought about by a special touch that reaches deep into the heart. The touch of Manjushri's sword of flames and of their light of realization transforms the seemingly hard facts of our life into the dream-like and mirror-like images that appear in the vast and boundless realm of awareness itself.

Manjushri is a metaphor for our firm and sustained intention to transform everything we experience into what it really is, a display of appearances in the mirror of awareness itself. He personifies our ardent and ever-mindful intention to see that everything is empty of an intrinsic, solid, and independent thingness-in-itself. He personifies the ability to see, immediately and as soon as something arises in our experience, that it emerges out of awareness itself—like a wave out of an ocean, like a sound in silence, like an event in stillness, like an image in a mirror, like a form in space.

What Manjushri and his sword mean can perhaps be best understood when we contrast him with the Greek mythic figure of

Atlas, who carries the weight of the world on his shoulders. His overburdened but also grandiose sense of self is us whenever we feel that we are carrying the crushing weight of our history on our shoulders. Manjushri is the opposite of Atlas. He lightens the load of whoever wields his sword of self-liberation. He dispels heavyheartedness and replaces it with a growing lightheartedness.

Practice

Sit down on a meditation cushion or a chair. Sit with dignity, with your back straight but not straining. Imagine a string attached to the top of your head, gently pulling up and straightening your back. You can do this meditation with eyes closed or eyes open, whichever works best for you.

Begin with the practice of becoming aware of the physical sensations of just sitting and breathing. Do this until your body begins to relax, and until your mind is less hyperactively latching on to and running after everything that appears in it.

Then shift your focus from the content of what appears in awareness to awareness itself. See if you can evoke a felt sense of the vast space in which everything appears. See if you can let yourself experience a felt sense of the stillness and the silence of that space. Or see if you can sense the non-reactivity of a mirror, or the feeling of an ocean-like expanse in which every experience arises like a passing wave. The goal in all this is to let these images or metaphors become directly felt realities.

Be patient with yourself in this. It does not happen right away. It will take time, possibly quite a bit of time. It takes repeated and sustained practice sessions before you begin to develop a directly felt sense of these images and metaphors. There is no need to become anxious about whether you can do this or not, because it is a universal capability. And there is no need to worry whether you are doing this right or not. Just do your best to follow the instructions and be patient. The rest will eventually begin to fall into place in its own good time. And it will do so in a way that is unique for you. There is no iron clad formula to make this work in exactly the same way for everyone.

Now imaginatively pretend to hold Manjushri's sword of flames. Touch all that appears in your awareness with the light of its flames. This sword is more your intention *than it is a thing. Touching everything that arises in your experience with this intention shows it for what it is, a dream-like appearance that is put on by awareness itself. All sensory experiences, all thoughts, all feelings, all automatic reaction patterns, all words, all doubts, including even all doubts about you doing this practice—all of it is transformed. It becomes what it always already is—not solid, hard facts but insubstantial fleeting experiences. If you like you can silently call everything that appears "a dream," or you can say "in a dream," or "empty," or some such phrase.*

Continue to do this until it becomes almost automatic, and until you develop a directly felt sense that "the world is awareness" and nothing else besides. This is a way to "wake up" from the dream of an independently existing personal self. It is how you wake up from the dream that would reify everything in your experience, most of all the feeling and the belief of having or of being a personal self.

As a result of this transformation everything now also stops being either likeable or unlikeable, good or bad. Instead, everything stands accepted and affirmed just as it appears. All judging reactivity stops. This is a practice of radical acceptance. Here, in this view and in this practice, everything looks perfect just as it is. The practice dissolves all usual unhappiness about things being as they are. Here all things are redeemed as they appear—just so, thus and such, and not otherwise. In the relative world of daily concerns you can and you should continue to pursue worthy goals and to avoid unworthy ones. But at this level of the more fundamental nature of reality everything is radically accepted as is.

With the touch of your sword of flames and the light of Manjushri's wisdom you dissolve the seeming solidity and factuality of all things. Most of all you dissolve the hardened beliefs and thinking habits of the unhappy personal self. That includes even all doubts or pessimism you may have about meditational self-care, and about your ability to learn it and to benefit from it.

Practice this until it becomes effortless and automatic or nearly automatic. Practice it until you no longer believe or need to believe anything you think. Until you recognize that everything you think is empty of any ultimate truth value. Practice until you recognize that, like a dream, everything, absolutely everything, is insubstantial. You can still appreciate the practical usefulness or the relative truthfulness of reasonably held beliefs, but you can let go of them as ultimate truths.

In a seemingly simple but profound way this results in you not taking yourself so seriously anymore. Without having to devalue or discredit your thoughts or feelings, or anything about your life, you begin to view all of it with a little more levity. There begins to be less of the usual heavy-handed seriousness. You are developing more lightheartedness about everything, perhaps even some mild but kindhearted amusement. That is a sign that your efforts are paying off. Your burdens become lighter as you throw off a great weight.

Francis of Assisi famously said: "Begin by doing what is necessary, then do what is possible, and soon you will be doing the seemingly impossible." Along similar lines the practice of "walking like an illusory being in a dream" says: "Begin by not believing everything you think, then practice not believing anything you think, and soon you will discover a lightheartedness you would never know if you had not suspended your habitual beliefs."

With the practice of touching everything that appears in your experience with the light of Manjushri's liberating insight, and with the practice of walking as an illusory being in a dream, you discover for yourself what has been said about the meditation tradition, that it is "a clever way to enjoy existence." You are now personally practicing this clever way to enjoy existence.

6

What's wrong with you? Nothing

View

"What's wrong with me?" To answer that question is the reason why many people turn to a psychotherapist. They have been struggling with an unbearable unhappiness they cannot understand, cannot explain, or cannot do anything about. But it is not only those who turn to psychotherapy who ask this question. It is a natural question of which every human being is capable. It often translates into: "Did I do something wrong? What am I do wrong? How can I change things? What can I do to make things better?"

The question is so natural, and the ground of normal unhappiness is so fertile, that it has been possible to build entire world-views—even cultures and civilizations—around the idea of there being "something wrong" with everyone. The West eventually developed around the foundational idea of an original "wrong," an "original sin." This idea—which is then often projected externally as the "wrongness" of other people—has been a major driving force at the heart of history. It has been used as justification for all manner of action against others. It has been applied at the level of individuals and at the level of groups, nations, and entire peoples.

For a Western mind it is extremely difficult to let go of notions of personal inadequacy. This is often first the inadequacy of other people, but in the end it is about its own inadequacy most of all. And seemingly paradoxically, the Western mind clings both unhappily and happily to its guilt and shame. It finds them to be the hardest things to let go of. For many people they are core elements of their self-definition. Take away their guilt and shame and they no longer know who they are. It is as if they were saying: "My guilt and shame are the last things I will ever give up. I will not let anybody take them away from me." Freud discovered this in what he called the patient's "resistance" to psychological treatment efforts.

"Original sin"—or every form of "What's wrong with me?"—is a primary target of meditational self-care. It is a core issue that is to be addressed with the approach of "Don't believe *anything* you think."

The belief in "original sin" and the focus on "what's wrong with me" usher in the associated belief that redemption or relief from unhappiness must lie elsewhere. It must lie in the future and in circumstances other than the present ones. It can only come after something about us has been changed, after we have become a new and improved person. Many people hope that psychotherapy can improve things in their current life. If that does not work they may place their faith in a religious notion of redemption in another life, after the current one, and by otherworldly means. Always the fundamental hope and belief rest in the future and in a situation different from now.

The almost compulsive scenario of looking to different circumstances in the future motivates nearly all action. It is the intention behind almost everything we do, from things as minor as scratching an itch to something much bigger, like looking for another job, another house, another career, or another partner.

The problem with an ideal state that lies in the future and that can only be found there is that it inherently makes the present moment less than good enough, even if only by comparison. That, in turn, consolidates the unhappiness that dreamed up the ideal future in the first place. It makes that unhappiness inescapable. As Nietzsche put it: "Wanting to go to heaven is an underhanded way to slander the earth." If being elsewhere than here and now is considered good and better, then being here now becomes not good enough, or bad.

Meditational self-care replaces the great weight of "original sin" with the lightheartedness of what the meditation tradition calls "original enlightenment." We do this in the most radical way, by renouncing the future and the obsession with the future. We renounce them in favor of the present. We learn to see that what we call "the present" is not a feature of linear time, squeezed between past and future, but a practice—an attitude and an intention. It is a practice of being fully present to the moment at hand. What one teacher calls "the power of now" transforms the unhappiness of "original sin" or personal "not-good-enough-ness" into lighthearted or enlightened cheerfulness.

The core meditation practice of learning to experience and accept each breath in just the way it comes and goes is the model for countering and lifting the great weight of "original sin." "Learn to love yourself," says Nietzsche, "so that you can stand to be with yourself," and so that you don't need to dream of another life, after the present one and elsewhere. In line with this the meditation tradition says: "Learn to love the experience of breathing, from moment to moment, so that you can learn to be happy with your life as it is—here and now, always here and now."

The focus on the always-changing and always-new experience of breathing is not for the sake of the breath itself and for breath-worshiping. It is for the sake of practicing the exquisitely fine art of being here, now, with this particular experience, whatever it may be, in this passing moment, and nowhere else. This radical posture replaces "original sin" with "original enlightenment." As already repeatedly said, this is something of which everybody is capable, but always only in the now of this precise momentary experience. It is always available now and never found later.

It does does not require that we first do something about ourselves or about the way things are right now. It is precisely by not wanting and not trying to change things that they stand redeemed—in their own glory.

Focusing on breathing is like boot camp for the mind. It teaches a core practice of being intimately present to the moment at hand. It provides the model for a basic strategy that is gradually applied to ever-larger areas of our life. Awareness of sitting and breathing leads to lightheartedness on the meditation seat. Radical awareness across an ever-widening range of experiences leads to a lightheartedness that becomes more sustained.

When we look closely at a tree we can see that no two leaves on it are the same. Each leaf is unique. It cannot really be compared to any other leaf. Looking closely it becomes clear that the very category of "leaf," the general abstraction we call "leaf," does not seem adequate to the uniqueness that is at stake. This abstraction can therefore not be applied. Looking ever closer we discover that the category of "leaf" simply falls away. This is radical practical philosophy and experiential science. It makes us see that, at a level of fundamental reality, we have to abandon the idea of a "leaf" as a familiar thing we can pretend to know. We have to let go of it as being just a thought, just another thought in awareness itself. Only then can we see just how every leaf presents itself. Otherwise its uniqueness is dismissed through a reductionism that fails to see it.

It is the same way with every breath, even with every separate moment of every breath. No two moments of breathing are the same. No two breathing cycles are the same. In the end we see that there is not even such a thing as "breathing" as a separate thing-in-itself. Paying close attention to just sitting and breathing we begin to see that these objects of meditation do not exist as separately identifiable things. There is only the endless stream of momentary experiences. In the practical world, such as that of a doctor's office, it makes of course good sense to speak of "breathing" as a process that deserves medical attention. But at the level of our deepest experiences and the fundamental basis of existence there is no such separate and independent thing as "the breath."

When we examine our experiences up close we discover something important. We discover that there is no such thing as a findable essential inadequacy, a definable and abstract not-good-enoughness-in-itself, an "original sin-in-itself." And so we can let go of the very idea of it, the belief in it, and the experience of it. This is true self-liberation.

What is left is the endless stream of moments of experience arising in awareness itself and nowhere else. Every passing moment is here automatically affirmed in radical acceptance. And we ourselves, with all our personal realities, are automatically and radically affirmed as well.

Enlightenment is discovering the capacity to be fully satisfied in this life and in this world—now, at this moment, one fleeting moment at a time, and not later. It is discovering the felt sense that, as Augustine put it: *"Sat est et bene est"*—"It is enough and it is good." The meditation tradition and meditational self-care make that experience possible in our life—as we have lived it, as we are now living it, and as we will go on living it.

Practice

Sit down on a meditation cushion or a chair, with your eyes open or closed, as you prefer. Sit with dignity, with your back straight but not straining. Imagine a string attached to the crown of your head, gently pulling up and straightening your spine.

Rest in just sitting and breathing. Make a mental body scan from the soles of your feet to the crown of your head and note all the physical sensations of which you become aware. Continue like this until your body becomes relaxed and your mind stops running after everything that appears in your awareness.

The goal in this practice is to look as closely as possible at each breath but without forcing your attention or anything else, and without any kind of effort. Simply follow the movement of each breath, in and out. Note the turning points where inhaling becomes exhaling, and where exhaling becomes inhaling. Look until the unique features of each breath become more clearly noticeable. Let every new breath be a brand new experience. Resist the inclination to control the breath or to change it in any way. Refrain from doing anything. Avoid comparing one breath to another. Let go of the very idea of breathing or the breath. Let each fleeting moment be as unique as it is.

Just let the body do the sitting and the breathing. Let go of thinking that you are the one who is doing the sitting and breathing. Let it just happen. Continue like this until it becomes clear that even the very notions of body, sitting, and breathing are not about three separate and independent things. Let these three words and concepts fall away.

There is no need to think about anything. There is nothing to figure out, nothing to question or analyze, nothing to interpret. There is nothing to be critical about. There is nothing to believe, nothing to understand, nothing to solve. There is nothing to worry about, nothing to plan. There is just sitting and breathing, and observing the sitting and breathing.

There is no audience to impress, there is no applause to be sought. There is only awareness of momentary experiences.

There is nothing to look for and nothing to wait for. There is nothing to make

happen in your mind or heart, and nothing
to prevent from happening. There is nothing
to aim for, nothing to achieve. There is
nothing to expect, nothing to hope for,
nothing to strive for. There is only awareness
of sitting and breathing, moment by
moment.

There is nothing to call good or bad,
nothing to reject or prefer, nothing to judge
good enough or not good enough. There is
nothing to compare. There is nothing to be
disappointed by. There is no right way to
breathe and no wrong way to breathe. There
is nothing to succeed in, nothing to fail at.
There is only open and accepting awareness
of just sitting and breathing.

Focusing on just sitting and breathing
without doing anything is the training
ground for the practice of not-practicing, the

meditation of not-meditating. It liberates us from the mind-made prison of an unhappy but dream-like personal self. It is the door to the vast and limitless space of awareness itself. It puts us in touch with the all-encompassing silent stillness that is awareness itself. It dissolves the small personal self. It makes us know that we are equal to the ever-present, boundless, and silent stillness that is awareness itself. It takes us to who we are at the level of our deepest nature.

7

An everyday practice: Slow down and do one thing at a time

View

Slowing down is a simple but powerful way to become content with where we are. It improves the quality of our life without first having to change anything about it. We practice it away from the meditation seat, and while we are engaged in our routine activities.

Slowing down takes us out of our preoccupation with the future, whether of the next moment or some more distant future after that. It repositions us in the present. This is where we always already are but where we naturally tend to forget we are. It stops us from doing what we are naturally inclined to do: imagining ourselves getting to the next moment or the next stage of our life. It counters the belief that these are more important than the present moment.

To be or not to be is not the question. We always already are, even while we may be pondering that very issue. To be in a hurry to get to the next moment or not to be in a hurry, that is the question. The question is whether we are going to slow down so we can really be where we are.

As already mentioned, a contemporary Zen master has described the meditation tradition as "a clever way to enjoy existence." This is no small claim, despite its beguilingly modest wording. Part of what makes it work is the practice of slowing down. Simple but not simplistic. And by no means easy.

Slowing down is a radical act. It is a declaration of independence. It sets us free from wanting to be where we are not— elsewhere and at a time other than now. It is a way to stop clinging to unhappy thoughts and feelings about the present that make us want to get away from it.

To see just how radical slowing down is we only have to try to do it. We quickly realize how hard it is to *remember* to do it. It is hard to remember to slow down because we are almost always already leaning into the next moment. Everything in our usual ways, including almost everything about our usual mindset, conspires to make us forget to slow down. But if we want to go fast and far on the path of meditational self-care we have to slow down in everything we do.

While our mind tends to get lost in things that are not happening it pays minimal attention to what actually is happening. Slowing down is the way to return to what is. It is the hallmark of true intimacy with our life. Being in a hurry toward the next moment and the one after that is avoidance of that intimacy.

The Zen Buddhist tradition has been defined as the practice of "doing one thing." That means doing one thing at a time. It means doing what we do with all our attention on it. That requires refraining from having a good part of our attention already focused on something else. It is the opposite of multitasking, and the opposite of running after every stick we see flying through the air.

Slowing down also means doing whatever we do for its own sake, not for a goal that lies outside of it and that comes after it. Pushed to its radical conclusion this means being willing to do what we must do for its own sake and its own sake only, and being willing to do it over and over again, endlessly. This is the equivalent of rethinking the myth of Sisyphus, who must eternally push a rock up a hill, only to see it roll down again so that he must always start over. Instead of imagining Sisyphus in abject misery over his lot of the eternal return of his rock and his job we must imagine him happy. We must imagine him content with what he is doing and has to do—this, here, now, always now, always this, always here.

The ultimate form of slowing down is stopping. That means not wanting to go further or elsewhere than where we are. This is the equivalent of the biblical creator of the world saying to the waters and the oceans: "You may go this far but not further." It means finding freedom even in the seeming unfreedom of accepting what is. It means accepting what is as it is, and learning to say and to feel: "It is enough, and it is good."

Stopping as the ultimate form of slowing down is also a way to understand the baffling idea of "dying before dying." This enigmatic phrase is about nothing other than being able to be content with things as they are at any given moment. It is a letting go of the need for a better future. That includes in the first place a letting go of the personal self, or "dying before dying," insofar as the personal self compulsively seeks a better future at the expense of the present. "Dying before dying" means nothing other than arriving in the present and discovering, at the level of our deepest knowing, that there is nothing that needs to be done about it. It is the spontaneous self-redemption of all that appears in awareness.

This is what the Buddha said and what he meant when he awakened to his state of enlightenment: "Everything is done. There is nothing else to do." From that point onward he practiced a form of meditation he called "nonmeditation." This is also the reason why Nietzsche, not unlike the Buddha, said of himself that he is "no improver of mankind." And it is why Lao Tzu, in the *Tao Te Ching*, said: "You want to improve the world? I don't think it can be done"—because it is already good enough and perfect as it is. And it is why the creation story of *Genesis* says that on the seventh day God rested because there was nothing else to do but see that the world is "good, very good." While social goals are of course worthy and important in the relative world of daily practical concerns, this has to be against a background of radical acceptance of how things are and came to be as they are.

Some or all of this may sound unreasonable, daunting, and unrealizable for us ordinary humans. It does not have to be so. Whatever may seem unreasonable, daunting, or unrealizable about it is the result of the personal self thinking about it in its usual ways. It is the result of the personal self feeling challenged to wrestle with it and to come out on top. The best way to look at these radical ideas and the best way to begin to practice them is to do so in small increments. This will be addressed below in the practice section of this chapter.

There are three elements in the practice of slowing down: attention, recognition, and appreciation. In reality these three elements blend together because they are ultimately one, inseparable. Looking at them separately here helps us see more clearly what is involved.

Attention here means that we decide and firmly resolve to focus on what we are doing at the very moment we are doing it. That means refraining from thinking about what comes next and thereafter, or about something that happened in the past. Attention is pure and unprejudiced interest. It is interest that looks and listens without preconceived notions, without imposing any prefabricated already-knowing. It looks and listens without automatically getting into position to react. As seen earlier, such attention has been called the soul's natural mystical prayer. We do not have to be a mystic or someone who prays or believes in a soul to understand what this means.

Recognition here means the opposite of handling the things that are involved in what we are doing in a thoughtless and mindless way. It means slowing down enough so we can acknowledge them as they present themselves in our awareness. It is about letting those things be fully present in our awareness, instead of being blind to them and treating them as if they were virtually invisible and not counting for much. It is the opposite of treating them like mere commodities to be exploited.

Appreciation means we recognize not only the presence of the things that are involved in what we are doing but also the fact that they have their own place in the world. It means seeing that they have their own origin, their own purpose, their own nature, and their own uniqueness.

When we practice slowing down in this way we can begin to see that even something as seemingly insignificant as a paper clip or anything else that happens to be at hand has its own surprising kind of wonderfulness. We do not have to be a poet, a philosopher, or a mystic to see this. Doing things more thoughtfully and ever so slightly more slowly is enough to make us begin to experience this inherent wonderfulness in each thing. We can do this without having to depend on the thoughts or words of poets, philosophers, or mystics.

Slowing down and stopping is also practiced in letting go of what is done and past. When we are done with something we have to be done with it. This makes of the act of forgetting a practice of letting go. It is a practice of not clinging to anything, a practice of nonattachment.

All of the above is easier said than done, because the mind of the personal self is extremely distractible. It sees baubles everywhere and it cannot resist reaching for them. As we have seen, it behaves like a hyperactive monkey jumping from one thing to another. The Buddhist tradition personifies distraction as the mythic figure of Mara. Mara is perpetually busy enticing the mind of the personal self with now this and now that. He is always offering something other than what is at hand. Legend has it that when the Buddha-to-be was on the verge of his great awakening Mara approached with his armies to derail the event. These armies are none other than the endless thoughts and impulses with which we distract ourselves. Mara tried to tempt the future Buddha with all manner of seductions. He offered worldly wealth and power, pleasures of every kind, even his own daughters.

The Buddha-on-the-verge-of-awakening responded to the seduction and the attempt at distracting him with the famous "earth-touching gesture." Seated in meditation he touched the earth with one hand. This gesture has been interpreted in many ways. Here, in this context, we can view it as the Buddha-to-be bringing himself back to here, now, this. That is to say, rather than letting himself be carried away by matters and promises of a different circumstance elsewhere he returned his attention to this, here, now. With that gesture the future Buddha made Mara and his armies of distraction powerless, and they walked away.

The Buddha later taught a method for disempowering Mara whenever he appears in our life, in the mind of our personal self. The method is simple but powerful. It consists of saying, "I see you, Mara," whenever some powerful thought, feeling, impulse, or mental state takes over and distracts our attention from being here, now, with whatever is present.

Saying, "I see you, Mara," is to be done not as fighting words but rather as a a benign acknowledgment of Mara's clamoring for attention. It is to be said in the same kind and friendly tone with which a mother speaks to a small child when playing peekaboo. The secret lies in not seeking to do battle with Mara. As Nietzsche put the same idea in his great philosophical New Year's resolution, and as seen earlier: "I do not want to wage war against what looks ugly. I do not want to accuse. I do not even want to accuse those who accuse. All in all and on the whole I want to affirm everything that appears." That affirmation is done without fighting with Mara. In contemporary parlance this is the practice of mindfulness: recognizing everything that appears in awareness without judging or doing battle with any of it, and then returning our attention to where we had placed it.

This practice of saying, "I see you, Mara," may be especially helpful in the morning, just as we are transitioning from sleeping to waking up. It is at this moment and through this door that unhelpful habitual thinking, feeling, and reaction patterns often enter our awareness and our day. We wake up worried, or in a grumpy mood, or unmotivated, or irritated and annoyed by the

things we know await us when we get out of
bed. This is a good time to routinely say,
"Good morning, Mara. I see you, Mara," as
soon as we get a whiff of these habits entering
our awareness and our day. Say it as you
would greet a kitten or a puppy or a toddler
wanting breakfast or wanting to play.

Practice

*The basic idea of this practice is
simple. Its difficulty lies in remembering to
do it. That is why it may be helpful to have a
plan for it and to do it with some discipline.
Pick one or two brief and uncomplicated
activities in which you engage every day.
Perhaps something like getting dressed, or
taking a shower, brushing your teeth,
walking to your car and getting into it, doing
the dishes, or any other routine activity you
can think of.*

Whatever it is you have chosen in order to practice slowing down, simply pay attention to the doing of it. Focus on the activity rather than on the personal self doing it. Focus on all the movements and physical sensations, and on all the things and materials involved. When your mind wanders, which it will, just as it does with the practice of meditative sitting and breathing, simply bring it back to what you are doing. Bring it back to the physical movements and sensations and to the objects involved. Simply notice them instead of, as usual, being almost oblivious to them.

As you focus on the activity you are doing, see if you can observe any aspects or features of the things involved that you may not have noticed before. That means becoming aware of things that are always present but to which you may not have been paying attention. It is a practice of making mini-discoveries. Nothing earth shaking as discoveries go, to be sure, but nonetheless something that is noteworthy in its own way and in its own right.

By doing this you are also beginning to practice appreciation of all that is involved in the activity. Such appreciation adds previously unnoticed value to the moment, to the activity, and to the materials and the things associated with the process. When you catch a sense of appreciation about anything in what you are doing, enjoy the pleasure of just dwelling on that for a few moments.

Practicing appreciation this way leads almost automatically and effortlessly to natural gratitude. Dwelling on gratitude for a few moments or minutes then almost automatically and effortlessly leads to the realization that everything that is good in your life you owe to other people or to circumstances or things not of your own doing.

When you practice slowing down you may find yourself unexpectedly wanting to stop in a moment of wonderment at the sight of something or other that you might normally just pass by unaware. Something never before noticed may suddenly speak out to you. This is like a kind of small-scale burning-bush experience, similar to the one Moses had, in the midst of an otherwise dull and perhaps mind-numbing desert of things not usually valued or even seen. Like a mythic burning bush in a desert this can be a moment when something speaks for itself without a need for words. When that happens, try not to break the spell of the

moment by adding any kind of silent
commentary.

This is where, as for Moses, ordinary
things can become truly unspeakable in their
mere and sheer presence. You do not have to
be Moses to experience this kind of burning-
bush presence. And you can even go beyond
Moses and directly experience that, at that
precise moment, in that precise experience,
you are yourself the very thing you are
looking at. For the usual limit where you end
and where the rest of the world begins falls
away here. You become as vast as the entire
universe. It is a moment in which, as one
poetic Zen master put it, a wave or even a
drop of water knows that it already is the
ocean.

You cannot make this kind of
experience happen by wanting it to happen.

You can only set the conditions for it, by ever so slightly slowing down. But that is all you are called to do. Anything beyond that is not for you to worry about or to do anything about. That is because this kind of experience is not the result of the activities of the personal self. It is a spontaneous and revelatory gift from awareness itself.

When, during the practice of slowing down, any kind of strong idea, feeling, impulse, or state of mind enters your awareness and threatens to distract you, silently say, "I see you, Mara." Do this in the way discussed above—patiently, kindly, like a mother with a small child. Or you can do it philosophically, with radical acceptance and without doing battle with what presents itself. This practice of saying, "I see you, Mara," or doing the philosophical equivalent of radical acceptance, is a practice and a meditational gesture that has to be repeated again and again, patiently and persistently .

8

Grandmother's ethics is more art of living than judgmental morality

View

Living contentedly depends on a practice that can be summarized this way:

Q: "How can I feel good about myself and my life?"

A: "By doing the right thing."

Q: "But what is the right thing to do?"

A: "What your grandmother would tell you to do."

This is a practical ethic for a happy life more than it is a moral-judgmental teaching about being good or being bad. It says what to do rather than what to be. It is a strategy for sustainable lightheartedness, not a doctrine for self-righteousness and for intolerance of what is judged to be wrong. It is useful because it tells us how to live, not what to think or what to believe. Philosophers generally make no distinction between ethics and morality. Here it is perhaps helpful to say that ethics emphasizes practices or doing while morality emphasizes value thinking and value judging.

The principle of doing "what your grandmother would tell you to do" is not just a learning tool for children. Its core method is also a central strategy in the multithousand-year meditation tradition. There it is called the "extraordinary method." It is a practice to help meditators achieve what their tradition calls the goal of "buddhahood in this lifetime."

That means awakening to enlightened awareness in this lifetime rather than in the very distant future, after countless more rebirths. Westerners can perhaps see this as redemption in this life and in this world, rather than having to wait for it after this life and in another world.

We are neither who we think we are nor who we think we would like to be. We are what we experience and do while we are experiencing and doing it. We are the result of our thoughts, our speech, and our behavior. We are what we are in what we think, in what we say to ourselves and to others, and in how we act. If we want to be content we must do more than moralizing. We must do more than thinking and talking about right and wrong, good and bad. We must practice doing what makes ethical sense. And what makes ethical sense? It is what makes us grow stronger in our best traits, rather than weaker. Consider this exchange between a grandmother and her grandchild:

Grandmother: "Two spirits are fighting each other in my heart. One tells me to do helpful things that make me stronger, the other tells me to do harmful things that make me weaker."
Child: "Which one wins?"
Grandmother: "The one that I feed."

Together these two mini-dialogues teach two essential principles. The second dialogue says that building a happy personality or character is done by doing what strengthens it and by avoiding what weakens it. It is helpful to bear in mind here that the word "ethics" comes from the Greek *ethos*, meaning "character." The second dialogue therefore talks about character development.

In contrast, the first dialogue says that knowing and remembering the difference between what strengthens us and what weakens us depends on having a clear image or model. By identifying with that image or model we can more easily know and remember what the right thing to do is.

This is the core of the "extraordinary method" of personal development through meditational practice. The tradition teaches a variety of techniques to implement this approach. These techniques are all more the same than they are different. The core idea is to form a clear and, most importantly, a deeply felt mental picture of the type of human being we want to emulate. Such an ideal model engages our interest. It energizes us and it helps us to sustain our attention. It inspires us with a felt sense of admiration, affection, and love. It makes us want to become just like the model.

Western psychology does not speak of an "extraordinary method," as the meditation tradition does. It speaks instead of the natural and spontaneous developmental process in which children "internalize" the image of a beloved parent. Without even thinking about it children internalize the experience and the mental impressions made by the admired and beloved parent. In this developmental process there is essentially no choice in the parental image that is being internalized. In contrast, in the meditation tradition this same process is applied to a deliberately chosen ideal model, often the Buddha or a Buddha substitute.

The general principle is this: We become what we "internalize." That is why children imitate and become like the parental figures as they experience them. They do so primarily in what those parents practice, and less in what they preach. This is a form of whole-person teaching and whole-person learning. It is more powerful than merely verbally based and intellectual teaching and learning. We learn more by what goes into the heart through direct experience than by what goes into the head through talking and thinking.

This explains why the word "believing" originally meant "beloving." It was a process of the heart first before it became a problem for the brain. Only in recent centuries did "believing" stop being "beloving" and did it become a process of the intellect and thinking. Only then did believing become a matter of whether there is or is not a provable correspondence between intellectual ideas about something and the reality of it.

The psychology of "internalizing" ideals is also why, as Nietzsche proposed, the stomach may be a better model than the brain if we want to talk about the mind. For the stomach is about "taking in" or internalizing what we put into ourselves—what we take on and take up and take in, what we taste, what we chew on, what we swallow, what we digest, what we metabolize, and what we make part of who we become. As some say, not without merit, we are what we eat, both literally and figuratively.

The traditional "extraordinary method" of developing ourselves as an ethical being is a practice of taking in the images and above all the felt experience of "beloved" human beings. This serves the goal of overcoming our less than happy personal self. We do this with an intake practice that amounts to a mental diet for more liberated and lighthearted living. This is the same reason why Nietzsche said that human beings are ultimately and evolutionarily meant to become "Overhuman" beings. The "Overhuman" is the man or woman who overcomes his or her personal dissatisfaction with existence by emulating larger-than-life models of enlightened cheerfulness.

The traditional instructions for the "extraordinary method" usually seem esoteric to the Western mind and taste. This is especially the case when they are presented in a language and using the imagery and techniques of the old texts. But when we examine these ancient instructions more closely we can see that they are essentially no different from modern image-based practices that are now widely used in the West. Here they are used in order to improve performance or progress in such fields as athletics, medicine, and psychotherapy, or in such areas as the training of pilots or soldiers. This image-based approach to teaching certain practices expedites the learning process. And so, as it is put in the meditation tradition, by the method of actively imagined but internally felt union with a model of an enlightened being "success in seeking enlightenment will not be far."

Psychologists have found that changing the images with which we form our sense of who we are changes our perception of reality. It changes our emotional experiences and our thinking process. It also changes our neurological, physiological, and behavioral response patterns. Those who understand this process and who learn to put it to work for themselves discover an important thing. They see firsthand that we create our personal realities from the combination of imaginable possibilities and our natural capabilities. Not accidentally, this is precisely how all natural self-hypnosis is defined. It is the spontaneous practice of creating personal realities from the combination of imaginable possibilities and our natural capabilities.

What the meditation tradition has been teaching for millennia and what Western hypnotists have also known for centuries is now doubly confirmed by the findings from neuroscience. They indicate that what we think shapes not only our experiences but even the very brain itself that provides the biological conditions or basis for those experiences. This means that we are constantly creating a brain that is tailor made to the uniquely individual life we have taught ourselves to live.

Natural self-hypnosis is not only a normal, natural, spontaneous, and defining human activity. It is an essential part of the human condition. As Nietzsche put it: "Man is always, at every moment, the as-yet-to-be-determined animal." That means we are always only half completed. We are forever becoming, rather than just being. We are continually completing the form we assume. We keep on doing this work of self-shaping or self-completion by what we think. And like Sisyphus we are never done with our work.

The question is not whether we should become interested in natural self-hypnosis or not. We spontaneously hypnotize ourselves all the time, whether we know it and like it or not. The question that matters is: Are we hypnotizing ourselves to create the life we want?

Self-hypnosis is a spontaneous and natural process that begins in childhood. We have no control over it for that reason. It is the developmental process that shapes our early and defining experiences. Thereafter it keeps on shaping our life as we live it, until we die. We have no choice in the matter of being self-hypnotizing creatures. The process is as inevitable and as necessary as breathing or having a heartbeat.

With the skill of deliberate and consciously practiced self-hypnosis, which we can learn in adulthood, we can shape our life according to freely chosen ideas or ways of thinking. These may well be different from those we learned in childhood. When we were children we lived by ideas and ways of thinking that go with being a child. But, as it is famously said, if we want to live as an adult we may need to shed our old and unfree childish ways in favor of freely chosen ones. This is why religions have rituals that initiate growing young people in the ways and beliefs of adulthood. And it is why we learn to practice meditational self-care.

Practice

This practice is done with eyes closed. Sit down on a meditation cushion or a chair. Sit with dignity, with your back straight but not straining. Imagine a string attached to the crown of your head, gently pulling up and straightening your back. Do a quick body scan and feel the physical sensations of just sitting and breathing. Then dwell in this physical awareness until your body begins to relax.

Now imagine someone you greatly admire for the profound dignity and for the universal decency of their humanity. It can be anyone you like, real or fictional. Or you can take the idea of someone you have heard about and you can make a mental picture of that person as you imagine them. The important point is that it must be someone whose presence would fill you with admiration and joy, someone whose qualities you want to develop in yourself.

Do not be shy here. Go all out and think big. Think in terms of ideals that can set the standard for all humanity and for all time. Perhaps someone like the Buddha or Jesus, or someone like Gandhi, Martin Luther King, Nelson Mandela, or Mother Theresa. Or it can be your grandmother, or a beloved teacher, or another person you admire and love. Make it someone who would be good for you and for all people to emulate. This is the first step in many contemplative traditions and practices that are meant to inspire us. These ideals make us want to develop and embody their dignified qualities and their universal decency in ourselves.

Thinking big is the first step in the so-called "extraordinary method" of the meditation tradition. Magnify and clarify this chosen image as much as you like and as much as you can. This is what the English word "magnificent" and the Latin "magnificat" mean. They refer to thinking big and to seeing magnificence. They encourage us to think big for ourselves precisely because of that magnificence. Religious and other spiritual traditions have more practical experience with this than most of us modern westernized people. We are often intimidated by or scared away from the practice and the habit of thinking big. Instead of being big thinkers we are often at risk of remaining small tinkerers.

Since you are learning meditational self-care you may perhaps find it especially helpful to do what the meditation tradition recommends. You may find it helpful to imagine a Buddha-type figure or person, in any way that you can.

Begin by imagining such a figure right in front of you. Review in your mind those characteristics of this figure that you want to develop in yourself. Evoke or generate a felt sense—not merely an intellectual idea—of these traits. Imagine yourself directly feeling, directly sensing, directly experiencing these traits in that ideal figure in front of you.

Then imagine that this figure begins to shine with a light that becomes brighter and brighter. Picture the figure dissolving in its physical outline and becoming a ball of pure bright light. Then visualize that ball of light moving toward you and hovering over the crown of your head. Next it descends, and it enters you through the crown of your head. Feel it enter into you, or just imagine or pretend that you feel it entering. It descends through your head and throat and upper chest area until it settles in your heart region. From there its light spreads through your entire body, every part of it.

Imagine the presence of that light in your entire body. Imagine or pretend you can feel it in your face, in all the muscles and fibers of your head, and throughout your entire body. Imagine yourself feeling like the ideal, feeling how it is energizing your insides. It has filled your body and taken on the form of your person. The ideal now lives inside you and you are identical to it. It is you and you are it.

Continue to sit like this, no longer as your familiar personal self but now as the model with which you have become identified. Sit like an embodied version or a new edition of the ideal model. The more often you repeat this practice, with a gradually increasing sense of the felt experience of it, the more you begin to become an embodiment of the qualities of this ideal.

When you get the hang of this practice you can expand its impact by imagining yourself feeling like this off the meditation seat. Imagine yourself feeling like this in familiar situations of your daily life and with the people who are part of it.

Begin this expansion with situations that are generally pleasant for you, and with people with whom you have friendly relations. Then, over a period of weeks and months, gradually expand this to a larger sphere of situations and people. Start with situations and people about whom you do not have strong feelings one way or another. Then gradually expand the sphere to situations and people who can sometimes be challenging for you. Then, ever so gradually, you can slowly include more and more difficult situations and people. This is how practitioners of the meditation tradition work on developing what they call their "buddhahood in this lifetime."

This is not magic. It does not involve superstitious beliefs, brainwashing, or blindly doing what someone else tells you to do. It is nothing but applied development psychology, the kind you have in any case been practicing on a daily basis since you were a child. Or, if you prefer, it is modern neuroscience put to work for you. For this is exactly how you have learned to think all the thoughts you have learned to think. It is how you have come to "belove" and to believe all your familiar beliefs. It is how you have developed all those personal traits and habits that are so deeply internalized that you are usually the last person to be aware of them, leaving it to other people to show them to you in their reactions to you. It is all this—except that now it is in the service of overcoming all manner of familiar personal unhappiness. It is for the sake of a sustainable contentedness and lightheartedness that give you a new kind of strength and that benefit not just you but everyone around you.

Anatomy of the unhappy personal self

This section could perhaps be placed at the beginning of the book, by way of introduction, instead of at the end. But that might encourage you to think that this teaching is in the first place aimed at your intellect, as informational material. But it is not intended as informational material, and it is not intended in the first place for your intellect. It is aimed at helping you develop personal, direct, and experiential knowledge. It is not about what somebody else has said or written. It is about what you can learn to see for yourself, based on your personal direct experience. It is meant to help you develop a way of knowing that does not depend on words and thoughts but on attentive personal observation. It is an invitation to engage in intimate personal inquiry into your experiences. This anatomy of the unhappy personal self is placed at the end in order to emphasize that it remains secondary to the personally conducted practices that precede it. At the same time it may serve as a guide to support you in those practices. Its subject matter is more for gradual realization than for preliminary information or factual exposition.

Think of this section as you would think of a guidebook for a walk in nature. The guidebook serves the experience of the walk, not the other way around. Walking comes first. In this teaching we are interested in one thing and one thing only: dissolving personal unhappiness. That is not something you do with intellectual information. You do it with practices that can free you from the monkey traps of the mind-made personal self, which is the source of all unhappiness.

With these preliminary considerations in mind, let us now turn to the matter of an anatomy of the unhappy personal self.

We are nowhere more unique than in our individual unhappiness. Since all personal unhappiness comes from identifying with self-images our unhappiness is unique because our self-imaginings are unique. There are nonetheless universal patterns that go into the process. It is therefore possible to outline a universal anatomy of the unhappy personal self. Becoming ever more aware of it as you continue to engage with the views and the practices described in this book helps you see and remove the obstacles from the path that leads out of unhappiness.

Most importantly, and before anything else, the personal self is always imagined as something that is separate from everything else. Everything else is experienced as other-than-self. It is not-self. The world is out there because I am here. I exist in my separate and unique selfhood, which is my identity. This natural and fundamental dualism is obvious when we think of it intellectually, but it is difficult to be aware of it in everyday life. That is because the obvious is often the hardest thing to see. It is even more difficult to see how this duality of self and not-self is the source of all personal unhappiness. It is especially difficult to see this on an ongoing basis and while we are going through our usual activities.

The dualism of self and not-self is the original form of all imaginable dualities. It lies behind every case of separateness. It gives rise to every form of this-versus-that. This format may range from the seemingly most benign or insignificant of twosomes to the most antagonistic and epic or biblical. It may well be as old as human consciousness. Not surprisingly, that fundamental opposition of self and not-self is reflected in one form or another in the mythologies of all major religions. In the Abrahamic religions it is imagined as *Satan* (in Hebrew, Latin, Old English), or *Satanas* (in Greek), or *Shaitan* (in Arabic). In all its forms this means "oppose" or "opponent"—or variations such as "obstruct," "adversary," or "enemy." It is imagined as the tension of opposition or the sense of separateness that permeates all thinking about reality and that makes the very activity of thinking possible. In the biblical myth of *Genesis* it is what causes human beings to be expelled from living in a paradise of innocence and peace. It is what lands them in a world of chronic unhappiness, longing, restlessness, and unending but futile toil.

Personal unhappiness arises with personal separateness. But conversely as well, and perhaps more surprisingly, personal separateness and personal identity require personal unhappiness. Bewildering and nonsensical though it may sound at first, the personal self needs its unhappiness. It will do anything to cling to it. Personal unhappiness guarantees the sense of separateness from everything that is other than the imagined self. It does so precisely by creating a sense of opposition. And so, as the ancient Greek philosopher Heraclitus said, "*polemos*"—war or conflict—is what makes the world go around.

I may complain about my distress and sorrow, and I may say and believe that I would do anything to be rid of them, but it is they that keep me being who I am and how I see myself and know myself. The personal self needs its unhappiness. Its unhappiness defines it and keeps it in shape and acting strong. It needs to be in opposition to something. Satan, the arch opposer who comes into being with existence itself, is necessary for my understanding of the world. Paranoia organizes the mind of the personal self and preserves its sense of identity.

What form does this arch opposer take in everyday life? The challenger is nothing more, but also nothing less, than the present situation, the moment at hand—life as it is right now. The personal self will always find something that is wrong with what is, or at least not quite right enough and in need of improvement. There is always something to be done about it so that we can get to the next and presumably better thing.

In all this the need for unhappiness requires unconsciousness about itself. We are naturally prone to being unhappy, and we naturally need things to be that way, but we also do not want to know about it. This makes the compulsion to hide ourselves behind fig leaves of every kind almost instinctive and inevitable. It is no accident that fig leaves play an important role in the biblical story of the expulsion from paradise. It says that, from the start, being human is being self-aware, and this is a source of distress resulting from conflict.

Since nothing in the universe ever remains the same from moment to moment the personal self is constantly faced with the challenge of having to adapt to change. This makes existence in an essential way satanic, plagued by an endless stream of obstacles that oppose our purposes at every turn. This perpetual but ever-changing Heraclitean war with what is means that the personal self must constantly struggle with something or other to maintain itself. This serves as a perpetual reminder that it is never complete, once and for all. It is therefore also never completely satisfied with the way things are, even under the best of circumstances. There is always something that needs to be added to or removed from the way things are. Or there is something that has to be done about it to change it in some other way. The personal self can never consider itself safe from challenges to its sense of identity. That identity is always and by its very nature precarious. It is in an almost constant state of disequilibrium. That is another factor that puts it permanently at odds with everything that is not-self.

It is easy to see how Satan becomes the personified image not only of everything that is not-self but also of everything that, for this very reason, represents evil. I am good, and I try to do good, but everywhere I turn I meet with opposition to all my good ideas, intentions, opinions, beliefs, plans, efforts, and actions. This is a bad thing. It is something that I can therefore rightly— meaning self-righteously—consider bad, or evil.

Things have been like this almost from the beginning, so Abrahamic mythology suggests. We humans have been feeding ourselves a mental diet made of the fruit from the tree of knowledge of good and evil. The claim to this knowledge has given us the fundamental dualism that is responsible for ending life in paradise. And so, by believing that we can know and that we do know the difference between good and evil we have lost our innocence and thereby also the life of harmony with the world. By feeding ourselves and everybody else this knowledge of what is good and what is bad we give ourselves a permanently restless heart condition, a *"cor irrequietam"* in the Latin of Augustine's Christian theology. Not surprisingly, it is often especially the priestly class that has contributed much to worldwide unhappiness precisely because it claims insider knowledge about good and evil.

Hand in hand with needing a sense of separateness the personal self also depends on a belief in linear time. It needs to believe in a past, a present, and a future. All three are, as Augustine wrote, mental constructs. The past is a product of memory, the present is a product of attention, and the future is a product of anticipation. Without sense of time the personal self cannot be. It cannot imagine itself without its defining story and its imagined future. The sense of time and of the personal self come about simultaneously. One cannot exist without the other.

The personal self needs in the first place a past. That means a story about itself. Without past, without history, it cannot recognize and know itself. Like Shakespeare's character of Bottom, from *A Midsummer Night's Dream*, it needs an account of what it has experienced. It wants to be able to tell its story, both to itself and to others. It needs that story for personal self-affirmation and for social role identification and acceptance.

But not just any story of past experience will do. The personal self needs an interpretation of what it has experienced but that interpretation must be rendered with poetic sensibility. It has to account for all the parts of its experience and it has to do so in a way that makes the personal self valued in its own eyes as it looks upon its history. That way the story and the life become worth telling. As Aristotle put this in his writings on poetic composition, the story of the protagonist in a drama, in this case the personal self, needs to be both confirmed and affirmed.

The need for a well-composed and well-edited biography speaks to what every human being desires most. The object of this greatest human desire is what the modern folk singer Melanie called "a good book to live in." For this is everyone's most fundamental yearning: "I wish I could find a good book to live in." As Nietzsche wrote: "We love life not because we are used to living [that would merely be the Darwinism of biological adaptation and survival], but because we are used to loving." And what do we in the end love most of all? The collected stories we tell ourselves about all that we experience in this world we inhabit our entire life.

The personal self does not only need a past but also a future. What captivates in all storytelling, including the storytelling involving the personal self, is the anxious anticipation about "What is going to happen next?" Even if the story has been good so far, things need to get even better or we become bored and disappointed. The personal self is always full of expectations that the future can and must be better than the present and the past. The ultimate version of this interest in "What is going to happen next?" is the need to believe in an afterlife that will hopefully be different from and better than life in the present.

The personal self believes that happiness lies in the future and that it therefore requires time to achieve it. First A has to happen so that B can happen in the future. Many cultures and traditions believe that achieving freedom from unhappiness takes time, usually a long time.

In everyday life it takes time before we can get to the next thing or to an improved situation. It takes a long time of growing up and of working on making a life that works for us. In self-care it may take years of psycho-therapy time. Here there may first have to be what can seem like ages of unsatisfactory experiences and therapy sessions before there can be any change or any light at the end of the tunnel. According to other cultural beliefs it may take many lifetimes, through many reincarnations. It may even take a time that lies altogether beyond historical time itself, in a realm of changeless eternity. But always this belief that happiness lies in the future, even if only in the next moment after we scratch an itch, is precisely what puts it beyond reach. For it puts it beyond the present, beyond how things are right now.

But No, so the meditation tradition teaches, in a radical departure from this futuristic view. Even though unhappiness has required time to construct, liberation from it takes no time at all. The very notion of time is precisely what gets in the way of liberation. The view of the meditation tradition says that seeking happiness, enlightenment, or salvation in the future prevents us from finding it where we are, which is always here and always now. This also means that all spiritual seeking, if that seeking looks to the future, is the very thing that gets in the way of finding what it is looking for. Differently put: Seek in the future and you will *not* find.

The personal self also believes that it has to do something before it can achieve its happiness. It believes that its goal can only be reached after that doing is done, after everything on one's list of things-to-do can be scratched off. By believing that its happiness depends on what it does for the sake of its future the personal self makes that imagined happiness depend on itself. It is considered a work product, a personal achievement, the fruit of our labor, and something that both confirms our story and that affirms its value, which we imagine and experience as positive self-esteem.

Nietzsche wrote that "man is always the esteemer." He is constantly evaluating all that he encounters and experiences. He puts the stamp of his evaluation on everything and then directs his actions accordingly. He makes endless lists of things that need to be done based on his "esteeming." The personal self believes that its unhappiness will last, and that there can be no final satisfaction, as long as any of its work remains to be done, as long as there continues to be a list of things-to-do. But No, so the meditation tradition since the Buddha has put it, it is precisely in not-doing, rather than in doing, that the unhappiness of the personal self is dissolved and that natural and deep contentment is refound.

Lightheartedness, so the meditation tradition suggests, is not something the personal self has to make happen or even can make happen. It is something to discover as already there. It is hidden behind the never-ending mundane concerns of the personal self. All it takes is walking through the doorway that gives access to it. This is a doorway we normally do not see because we keep it hidden from ourselves. And we keep it hidden by standing right in front of it and keeping our back turned to it.

The personal self looks to the future for its happiness but it is at the same time filled with anxiety about the future. Simultaneously hoping for better experiences in the future and fearing that bad things may come from it puts the personal self in a position of being forever anxious. It is stuck between the rock of wanting something and the hard place of fearing something that comes from the same source. This makes the future both promisor of all that is considered good and executioner of all that is feared as bad. That makes the future look both potentially heavenly and hellish. And so we have the myths of heaven and hell to match.

The personal self, in its focus on the future, implicitly thinks that the present is not good enough. It is the opposite of Augustine's *"sat est et been est,"* "it is enough and it is good." The personal self cannot tolerate letting things be as they are. It nearly always needs to change something about what is. This reactive need to change things as they are is, in the Buddha's language, *dukkha*. This is traditionally translated as suffering or unsatisfactoriness, or, more broadly, unhappiness.

The present is primarily used as a stepping-stone. It is treated as a transitional phase that must lead to something other and better than itself. This elevates transitional dissatisfaction and implicit nihilism about the present to a permanently nihilistic view of it. Some say: The best is yet to come. That means the present does not compare all that well with the promised better future.

We invariably imagine the happiness for which we strive in a place and time other than where we are. The present is devalued and diminished in importance as soon as we look away from it to the future. The image of our ideal future self, always pictured as happier than we are right now, is precisely what brings our unhappiness with the present and with ourselves into being. This leads, on a more absolute or extreme scale, to the longing for an altogether different world, an other-than-worldly world, a heavenly world.

Since the personal self has little interest in the present for its own sake it does not pay much attention to it beyond the impulse to get past it and to the next moment. What attention it does pay to the present is focused on what needs to be changed about it, and on what has to be done to bring that change into being.

The greatest good for the personal self is often projected at the greatest distance— both in time and in degree of differentness from the present. The further out it lies in the future the better it must be. For many the greatest good is projected beyond life and beyond this world.

Because of its deficit in attention to the present the personal self is a poor observer of what it sees, a poor listener to what it hears, and a poor reporter of what it senses. It does not see much of what is present, it does not hear much of what is being said, and it misperceives and misreports much of what it senses. Instead, and more often than not, it almost immediately takes up a reactive and argumentative posture in relation to what it sees, hears, and senses. This is the original and satanic oppositionalism once again. It may assume different forms. It can be at the level of a contrarian personal opinion about something, or it can assume pretensions of absoluteness at the philosophical level of things, or it can take on every imaginable form of opposition in-between. While the self appears to be looking, listening, and noting what it experiences, it is already formulating its preconceived opinions, its personal views, and its already-knowing.

The personal self is goal oriented. Its operational manual is the list of things-to-do-today. It does not like to just sit and to just breathe, which is why these simplest of things turn out to be as difficult as they are. The mind of the personal self does not readily tolerate just sitting and just breathing. It keeps on throwing sticks in the air for the personal self to chase after. And so the personal self always wants to be doing something—about the situation at hand or about the ideas that come to mind. Because the present is only a stepping-stone to the future and not satisfactory in itself nearly every moment seems to call for an action plan. One must have an ambition and a goal. The best goals must be measurable. They must be evaluated with outcome studies.

The present tends to be valued only as a commodity, serving the needs of the imagined and happy future self. But even though the future seems to be promising, once the personal self gets there that future becomes itself present. There is no other time to be than in the present. The future-now-made-present is then once again not good enough and not satisfying.

The personal self is perpetually reaching for something that is felt to be lacking. Its perpetual torment and lament is: "Don't have enough. Need more. Need different." This is what, in the language of the Buddha's teachings, is called *tanha*, thirst.

The personal self perpetually feels incomplete, unfinished. It is forever looking for an addition that will improve it, but the work of improving is itself never done. This solidifies the sense that the personal self is never quite good enough. It reinforces the belief in its inadequacy—its "original sin."

The personal self is focused on results. Results are measured by how they change the present and by what they do for the future self. In contrast, habitual and often seemingly compulsive and eternal returns of the same experiences, for no other apparent sake than their recurrence, is how the mind-made self imagines the perfect hell.

223

Nothing could be more demonic than having to live this moment and this life over and over again, in an eternal return of the same things without any changes. We have a good idea and a perfect picture of just how demonic and hellish this is thought to be. We personify this form of existence and we talk about it as the myth of Sisyphus. He must forever push a boulder up a hill, only to see it roll down again and again, so that he must endlessly start over, never to be done with his labor. As Nietzsche wrote about this Sisyphean plight, which we all share in our compulsively returning experiences and in our fixed reaction patterns to them: "We know that we are being fooled [in thinking the future will bring relief as a result of our action], yet we lack the power not to be fooled."

The personal self is never fully and finally satisfied by any of the results it achieves. There may be temporary moments of success and satisfaction, to be sure. We have what Nietzsche's fictional Zarathustra calls our "little pleasures for the day and for the night." But after a while they too stop satisfying, if for no other reason than that everything in the universe is forever changing. When a temporary pleasure wears off something else is needed and we go in search for it. That way we may find the next pleasurable thing. But it too will only satisfy partially and temporarily.

The personal self is perpetually prone to being impatient with the way things are. It easily becomes intolerant in the process. This sets the stage for a potentially chronic and almost existential irritability with the state of the world. It also feeds an equally chronic, even if ever so subtle, hostility toward things as they are, here and now. Oppositionalism once again, eternally.

The personal self feels entitled to something better than what it has. This is considered a birthright. It includes the right to better oneself, now also guaranteed by constitutional law. In practice that means: Do not even think about accepting what is. This, in turn, is often translated into: Be angry, complain, demand change, claim victimhood. Without a virtually constant stream of complaints—even if silent or if so subtle as to be barely noticed—the personal self cannot maintain its sense of identity. If man is always "the esteemer," as Nietzsche said, he is also the perpetual complainer, even if he is civil and diplomatic about it.

The personal self thinks in terms of right and wrong. It is obsessed with this founding dualism. The ideals one has for oneself are what is right. Everything else is different and therefore cannot be truly and completely right. By implication it is essentially wrong, even if that thought is cast in the sweetest language. Everything is in need of judgment and advice, both of which the personal self is willing to provide. And having been raised on a diet from the fruit of the tree of knowledge of good and evil, the personal self knows what is good for one and all.

The mind-made self also tends to believe that it has been wronged. This makes it into a mini-version in everyday life of the biblical Job. He speaks and eventually shouts to the heavens to demand an explanation and justification for his unhappiness, which he did not deserve. The unhappy self, like its archetypal representative Job, believes that things should be different from the way they are. Why are they the way they are? Who or what is responsible? Who or what is to blame? We should not have been wronged. We should not have to accept any wrongs.

Because it feels wronged the personal self acts as if entitled to be in bad moods of every sort. Job's biblical anger and rage are the bad mood of the unhappy self writ large. The personal self is prone to become stuck and immobilized in its angry and rageful unhappiness. Even while it may outwardly appear quiet it may be silently screaming bloody murder in protest over its undeserved unhappiness. But it may also be, and it often is, inwardly unaware. Without knowing it the personal self may be settling for what Thoreau called a life of "quiet desperation."

The personal self often thinks or acts as if it is worse off than others. This is the subtlest formula for strengthening one's unique sense of identity: to be a greater victim than others. The personal self has other ways as well to compare itself to others.

It often feels and acts superior. The ideal it has for itself is different from and better than what is given in the present moment. It takes this ideal as reference point and as measure of all things. And it is always comparing. As Nietzsche put it, it is always "esteeming." It is not only superior to all other personal selves. In its imagined ideal and future form it is also superior to its own self-of-the-moment. But this reinforces its discontent of the moment, its unhappiness with life as it actually is at this moment.

The personal self also, and at the same time, tends to feel inferior. This results from forever living in a tiresome present that is never quite good enough. The never-quite-good-enough present confirms that the self must be inadequate in its core. "Original sin" has infinite ways to present and preserve this sense of inferiority. And it does so even while the personal self is forever busy trying to mask the feeling and the appearance of inadequacy with fig leaves of every sort.

The personal self easily and often feels guilty and ashamed. It uses guilt and shame as the last and firmest bastion to defend its delusion of separateness. That way the feeling and belief of having a separate and independent identity can not be easily challenged. For in my guilt and my shame I am most uniquely and most unassailably me.

Nobody can take them away from me. Nobody should even think of trying.

The personal self naturally tends toward xenophobia, a reflexive dislike of or prejudice against people who are strangers and other than oneself. It is prone to entering relations of strife with whatever and whoever is different. It dislikes and fears what is not-self. It is perpetually ready to wrestle, in an endless *polemos* or struggle that is at heart of biblical proportion. Whether it is the struggle of an individual against something that is not-self, the struggle of a people fighting oppression, or the struggle of the biblical Jacob wrestling all through the night with an unknown stranger, it is always in some fashion a struggle born of xenophobia.

The mind-made self is constantly comparing its achievements to those of others. This makes it prone to envy, in the same way that demigods are envious and resentful of real gods. Someone else may have what the personal self wants but lacks. That other self may therefore be better or think itself better. This must not be tolerated. Something has to be done about it.

The personal self believes that it cannot exist without thinking. It needs thinking for its self-definition and for its self-preservation. Beyond that it needs to think and have an opinion about everything that crosses its mind and its path. It tries to know everything about everything, or at least as much as necessary to form an opinion.

The personal self believes that thinking is the originator of all understanding. It does not realize that thinking often comes last, not first. It tends to come last as the reactivity that serves to justify and preserve the personal self in all that it does and in all that it cherishes. Thinking is often more about following than leading. The personal self follows and attaches itself to what the meditation tradition calls initial and unelaborated thought, which arises spontaneously in awareness. The personal self then elaborates on this initial thought and becomes identified with this elaboration, which is calls thinking.

In contrast, the liberated self, the more lighthearted and more cheerful self, has fewer and fewer opinions. It does not always need to know more and to have more information. It does not have to think about everything anymore. The unspoken prayer of every meditator is: "Deliver me from thinking." He or she seeks refuge from thinking. But this is not anti-intellectualism, and it is not withdrawal from reality or the end of concern about reality. It is liberation from unhelpful compulsive thinking that reifies the belief and the felt sense of having or being a personal self.

Practical thinking about the realities of everyday life remains when one abandons thinking that reifies the self. It remains even for the meditator who is freed from belief in a personal self. But now there is no longer a need to think more than is necessary. The more lightheartedly cheerful self lives on a diet of reduced thinking and a reduced need to have opinions about everything. It knows less and it thinks as little as possible. It begins to spend more time resting in peace. Above all it learns to rest in peace here and now, in the moment and the situation at hand. It no longer seeks peace elsewhere and later, in the future or after its life ends.

The more lightheartedly cheerful self not only has fewer opinions but it also does not necessarily believe in them any longer. It says "Maybe" often, including and in the first place about its own opinions. It knows less than it used to think it did. It no longer believes that it is as smart as it used to think it was. Instead of endlessly thinking and opining the liberated self begins more and more to fall in love with everything it encounters and just as it is. It does so wordlessly and without thinking. It does so like a baby who falls in love with a mother's face, or like a grandmother who falls in love with a grandchild. It does so, the meditation tradition says, like a child who falls in love with all the images and colors and everything it discovers when it first enters an ornate temple. This is not love out of need and greed or the thirsting of *tanha* but love out of awe, delight, admiration, and adoration.

Liberation from the unhappiness of the personal self begins with radical acceptance of what is. Hence the instruction to "Sit. Just sit." This simple yet difficult practice is the traditional core and the model of all forms of radical acceptance. It is the strategy of not-doing that led the Buddha to discover and to say that the ultimate form of meditation is nonmeditation. But, let there be no mistake, it took the Buddha six years of meditating to achieve the practice of nonmeditation. Like every so-called overnight success the Buddha's liberation was years in the making.

Liberation from unhappiness means both freedom from desire for anything and freedom from fear of anything. Nothing is needed because the present is enough as it is.

To use the Latin words of Augustine one more time, "*Sat est et bene est*"—"It is enough and it is good." For everyday practical living the concerns of the moment and of future needs remain useful. But at a more absolute level the idea of needing anything falls away. Similarly, fear of the future falls away as well. By being attentive to the present the notions of time and future fall away as a cause of fear, worry, hope, or concern. In the Buddhist tradition a liberated person is therefore sometimes given the honorific name and title of "*Jigme*"—"Fearless."

The most radical acceptance practice is acceptance of absolutely all the experiences of the personal self—including all experiences pleasant, unpleasant, and neutral. With this kind of radical acceptance the mind-made self comes to be seen as having depended even on its unique unhappiness in order to get to where it finds itself now, at the gate of liberation from every unhappiness.

This most radical form of radical acceptance includes even the very notion and the very experience of a personal self. But now this personal self is no longer seen as a hard and solid fact or thing, a separately and independently existing entity. It is now seen as a manifestation and expression of something larger than itself. It is seen as a manifestation and expression of a vast and boundless awareness that makes the mind-made self and all its experiences possible in the first place—and necessary.

The personal self would not be able to arrive at radical acceptance without the unhappiness that made the very discovery of such acceptance necessary and possible. The personal self owes a debt of gratitude to its unhappiness. On this the Buddha in ancient times, Nietzsche in modern times, and many philosophers in-between agree. When the personal self discovers that debt of gratitude the unhappiness dissolves of its own accord. It dissolves automatically and spontaneously, without the personal self having to do anything. This is what the Buddha meant by the practice of not-doing.

Radical acceptance does not take a long time to achieve, even though it may be long in coming. And while it may be long in coming it is nonetheless not to be looked for in the future. It can only happen here, now, in this moment, in the situation and the circumstances at hand. It happens through fully absorbed attention to the present as it is. Developing private unhappiness takes the time of one's drama and history but acceptance takes no time at all.

Acceptance, possibly long in coming but taking no time in happening, is sudden. It is spontaneous and complete. This is just how Job discovers it to be when he falls silent in his complaints about his unhappiness. He falls silent when the ever-present miracles of the world are suddenly all that he sees everywhere around him. He sees them as if for the first time, even though they have surrounded him all along. He receives no answers in his demand for understanding. He does not become smarter. He does not end up giving wise teachings and writing wise books. Instead, he enters silent awareness itself. That ends all demands for understanding. It also ends all demands for justification of his existence and his experiences.

The personal self, then, thanks to the unhappiness against which it has struggled all along, discovers that this very same unhappiness is itself, and paradoxically, the hidden door that opens up to liberation. Unhappiness opens up to boundless awareness when the personal self practices acceptance of what is. It opens up when the self practices not-doing. That means in the first place not-thinking. As the language of the major religions, wisdom writings, and contemplative traditions of the ages puts it: The kingdom of heaven does not lie elsewhere, or in some future time, or in an afterlife, or in another world, but in the way things are here and now.

Precisely by accepting what is and by not doing anything do we discover that the personal self does not need to be unhappy anymore.

A final word: Do not expect applause

An ancient mind-training manual that is still used today lists a multitude of practices to overcome the natural unhappiness of existence. Its last point is simple and blunt. It says, "Do not expect applause."

In other words, do not engage in these practices in order to receive public approval. That much is obvious. But there is more. The last point, which applies to meditational self-care as well, is that the practice must be done for its own sake and for no other reason—just as music is practiced for its own sake, and just as all art is practiced for its own sake. Meditational self-care is an art in its own right. It is the art of everyday conscious living with more lightheartedness and enjoyment of existence. Not only is it not to be done for the sake of social approval. It must not even be done for the sake of self-validation.

Most importantly, the practices are aimed at dissolving our attachment to the idea of a personal self. They are meant to awaken us to awareness itself as a basis from which to operate. That means liberating ourselves from the monkey traps of ideas about ourselves. It means learning to access and develop more lightheartedness and gaining freedom from heavyheartedness. In the process this also and automatically, without us having to do anything, benefits others. For it has a positive effect on the social aspects of our way of living.

If you find yourself looking for something that lies outside of the practice then your understanding of it needs itself to be resubmitted to the practice. Hence the instruction which the Zen version of the meditation tradition prescribes: "Sit. Just sit. Nothing more to do." The primary practical goal is to free you from being lost in thought.

In making these teachings your own, try to eventually remember the descriptive titles of the practices. Contemplate and rehearse them until you can recite them as easily as someone might recite the commandments of their religion. Except that they are practically useful suggestions but not commandments. Make them your own, each separately and all of them together. Understand what they are about and what they are for. That way you will have a map to navigate all the experiences and all the events of your entire life, no matter what the conditions you are facing. Turn this teaching into your own "clever way to enjoy existence."

Postscript

If you find that this book offers something that sounds potentially helpful to you, and if you are not already engaged in an ongoing meditation practice, then it may be a good idea to consider finding a reputable meditation teaching center with a strong traditional background. That way you will have access to further guidance. Doing things entirely alone is not impossible but unnecessarily difficult and, more likely than not, less effective.

Whether you seek a teacher or not, it is necessary to become ever better acquainted, and ever more familiar up close in your own and direct experience, with the profound insights that have come out of the Buddhist meditation tradition. At the same time, be open to the insights from other ancient traditions and from Western thought that have spoken of the same things. The practice of meditation has to be continually infused and enriched with the wisdom of these insights. It must also be enhanced by everyday behaviors and an ethic that have been informed by them. But remember that you do not have to "become a Buddhist" in order to benefit from the teachings and practices in this book.

Developing a meditational self-care practice takes time, patience, persistence, and determination—like learning to play a musical instrument, as already mentioned. It is the work of a lifetime. A good practical goal to aim for is simply, but by no means simplistically, to "get used to practicing" and then to keep on practicing. The rest mostly takes care of itself.

Further reading

Batchelor, Stephen. *Buddhism Without Beliefs*

Bodhi, Bhikkhu. *The Noble Eightfold Path: Way to the End of Suffering*

Brach, Tara. *Radical Acceptance*

Brunnhölzl, Karl. *The Heart Attack Sutra*

Chapelle, Daniel. *Nietzsche and the Buddha: Different Lives, Same Ideas*

Chödrön, Pema. *When Things Fall Apart*

Gethin, Rupert. *The Foundations of Buddhism*

Goldstein, Joseph. *Mindfulness*

Harvey, Peter. *An Introduction to Buddhism*

Kornfield, Jack. *The Wise Heart*

Mitchell, Stephen. *The Book of Job*

Nanamoli, Bhikkhu. *The Life of the Buddha*

Salzberg, Sharon. *Real Happiness*

Sluyter, Dean. *Natural Meditation.*

Surya Das. *Awakening the Buddha Within*

Suzuki, Shunryu. *Zen Mind, Beginner's Mind*

Thich Nhat Hanh. *Interbeing*

Thubten, Anam. *No Self, No Problem*

Tolle, Eckhart. *The Power of Now*

Trungpa, Chögyam. *Cutting Through Spiritual Materialism*

Wallace, B. Alan. *The Seven-Point Mind Training*

About the author

Daniel Chapelle is the author of *Nietzsche and the Buddha: Different Lives, Same Ideas – How Nietzsche May Yet Become the West's Own Buddha* (New York: Peter Lang, 2020); *The Soul In Everyday Life* (Albany, NY: SUNY Press, 2003); *Nietzsche and Psychoanalysis* (Albany, NY: SUNY Press, 1993). Forthcoming books are *The Necessity of Unhappiness* and *Karma for Westerners*. He received his doctorate in psychology from the Institute of Philosophic Studies at the University of Dallas. He has more than thirty years of experience in clinical psychological consulting and practices Indo-Tibetan meditation.